Trial by Trail

Trial by Trail

BACKPACKING
IN THE
SMOKY MOUNTAINS

Johnny Molloy

The University of Tennessee Press • Knoxville

All photographs are by the author.

The paper in this book meets the minimum requirements of the
American National Standard for Permanence of Paper for Printed
Library Materials. ∞ The binding materials have been chosen
for strength and durability.

Library of Congress Cataloging-in-Publication Data

Molloy, Johnny, 1961-
    Trial by trail : backpacking in the Smoky Mountains / Johnny
Molloy. —1st ed.
        p. cm.
    Includes bibliographical references.
        ISBN 0-87049-913-0 (pbk.: alk. pa.)
    1. Backpacking—Great Smoky Mountains National Park (N.C. and
Tenn.)—Guidebooks. 2. Hiking—Great Smoky Mountains National Park
(N.C. and Tenn.)—Guidebooks. 3. Trails—Great Smoky Mountains
National Park (N.C. and Tenn.)—Guidebooks. 4. Great Smoky
Mountains National Park (N.C. and Tenn.)—Guidebooks. I. Title.
GV199.42.G73M65 1996
796.5'1'0976889—dc20   95-4393
                                                            CIP

For Allison, R.C.M., and all those
with whom I have shared a campfire
in the Smoky Mountains

Contents

Illustrations

Preface

In the school of the woods,
there is no graduation day.

—Horace Kephart,
Camping and Woodcraft, 1917

Leaning against the gray rock outcrop, I scanned the horizon. There the contours of rolling ridges softened and melted into sky. A grassy cove was clearly visible below. Ants marched diligently amid the tall grass at my feet, building a small mound with freshly dug dirt. A light breeze drifted through the trees nearby. Dark thunderheads to the west promised rain.

Precipitation surely had been a force in shaping these old, old mountains. Suddenly I realized that similarly these mountains had shaped *me*, during the decade I had spent discovering the wonders contained in the Great Smoky Mountains National Park. Had I learned more about the land or about myself? The answer did not matter; I was better off for the experience.

This book is a collection of true backpacking adventure stories, tales of trial by trail. During the trials recounted here, I grew as a denizen of the outdoors and as a human being. The more I learned, the more I wanted to learn. The more, too, I realized how much there was to discover, both within the Smokies and within myself.

In the beginning, backpacking was utterly foreign to me. I was a flatlander, born and bred in West Tennessee, and I never had known or cared that my home state had mountains, bears, and trout streams. Part of the television generation, I was pre-occupied with socializing, sports, and chasing girls. This did not change when I came to Knoxville and the University of Tennessee in the fall of 1980. I immersed myself in campus activities centered around frolicking and football.

In the latter part of my first year, I met Calvin Milam. We became fast friends and rented a house together the next fall. An avid backpacker from Chattanooga, Calvin went off to the Smokies from time to time. I stayed in town, sleeping in beds and going to bars.

One morning when the Crimson Tide of Alabama was in town for the year's biggest football game, I was surprised to see Calvin loading his backpack. "Aren't you going to the game?" I asked.

"No, I'm going backpacking in the Smokies," he replied. Then, as now, I held Calvin's ideas in high regard. I made a vow to try this outdoor hiking sport.

That very first trip evoked in me a passionate first love—for the wilderness that lives within everyone. My love affair with the Smokies, like any relationship, encompassed many mistakes. And the mountains can be very unforgiving. Certain decisions I made in the beginning seem foolhardy now. But only through risk does one accumulate valuable experience. And no matter how many helpful guidebooks one reads, there is no substitute for experience in a truly wild place such as the Great Smoky Mountains National Park.

National parks are very special places. These areas are supremely beautiful or have rare ecosystems or other unique features. Such attributes need protection, which comes in the form of regulations. In my early backpacking days, I saw these strictures as an impediment to my personal use of the mountains. I violated the rules insolently, as this book too well demonstrates. Now I shudder at the memory. My own experience in the Great Smoky Mountains National Park and seeing others violate rules brought me full circle, turning me into an upholder of park regulations. I am now a volunteer in the Adopt-a-Trail program that thrives on the Tennessee side of the park.

Wilderness exploration is inherently a risky activity. No wilderness is without risk, and without risk there would be no wilderness. The key is to minimize risk. A day or a week traveling in the wilds entails a series of individual steps, decisions that must be made to complete the journey from beginning to end.

Crossing a creek suggests the decision-making process. To continue your journey, somehow you must cross a certain creek. Should you rock-hop or wade? If you rock-hop successfully, your feet will stay dry and time will be saved. But the rocks are slippery and you might fall in, getting wet and twisting an ankle or suffering more serious injury. But the outcome might be worse than that. You might find a decent route that would take you 90 percent of the way and then be faced with a final jump of five feet onto a mossy rock at the water's edge. It is winter, too, so a fall into the water could lead to hypothermia. Once the cold begins to affect your thinking, you might make still poorer decisions.

Wading is the second option. It goes more slowly; there are no jumps to make with thirty-five shifting pounds strapped to your back. Yet wading certainly will involve getting wet. It is winter, remember? A stout limb would help you maintain your balance while crossing the swift waters. Water depth must be gauged from the bank. It looks like it is not more than knee-deep. The water temperature cannot be much above freezing, which means that, upon entering the creek, distracting pain and then numbness will set in, adversely affecting your crossing ability. Crossing barefoot will keep your shoes dry, but you might injure your toe, slamming those numb feet into an unseen rock. The creek bottom is sure to be slick. The crossing will be safer with booted feet; your shoes will be sodden, but your upper body, backpack, and its contents will more than likely stay dry. And since this is a winter hike with days to go, keeping your sleeping bag and other gear dry is more important than saving time. You have two extra pairs of socks to change into at camp. To minimize risk, you decide to cross the creek with boots on but taking your socks off, keeping them dry, and putting them back on after the crossing.

All the outdoor guidebooks advise making sure not to cross

a moving body of water above a waterfall. You have studied the
water below and above, choosing the safest route. Your read-
ings also have taught you to loosen your pack as you cross, so
that you can ditch it in case it holds you under water after a
spill. A fittingly stout limb has been selected, to use on the
creek bottom to steady yourself. You also remember to face upstream for better balance.

As you enter the bone-chilling current, your stomach starts
to churn. The urge to bolt across and get it over with is nearly
overpowering. Sharp pains climb your legs; one false move could
be injurious. That one thought helps you keep your cool, and you
make it across slowly, surely, and safely. A sense of triumph
sweeps over you. You have built confidence for the next decision. Your journey can continue. *That* is minimizing risk.

Take the same situation six months later. It is August; the
temperature is nearly eighty degrees. The creek flows at half the
winter level. Rocks, smooth dry ones, are exposed that were not
before. Stopping at the water's edge, you make a quick survey
and plot an easy rock-hopping route. You loosen your pack
straps, then you are on your way. But, while crossing, you are
struck by the water's cool clear allure. So, on the other side, you
fling your pack to the ground, strip naked, and splash in the
mountain stream. That is *fun*.

Certain sections of this book deal with whitewater canoeing, off-trail hiking, and solo backpacking. Each of these
activities poses a new set of challenges and risks that require
thoughtful decision making, for a wrong move may have grave
consequences. Grave consequences entail even weightier decisions, with less pleasant options. Thus it is crucial that you use
your head as well as your physical skills in such undertakings;
assess your outdoor experience and physical capabilities, and act
accordingly!

As a novice, I sometimes took foolish chances, got in way over
my head, and made mistakes. A few more false moves along the
way, and I might not be here to tell these tales. But I am. If you
feel uncomfortable as you visualize yourself doing something I

did, then that is one experience you will not have to go through the hard way.

As a sport, backpacking is delightfully free of dogma. There are as many opinions on the best way to backpack as there are backpackers. Unlike sports such as basketball, no rulebooks exist on how to hike. Trail treaders will disagree even about something as important as a list of essential items always to have on your person. Each trip has its own requirements. You are not going to take shorts along on a three-night winter hike in the high country, or wool gloves in the summer. Wise backpackers assess their gear needs for each situation before leaving home.

It is also possible to go without and adapt. That is how I discovered that many "necessities" really are not necessary. People underestimate their ability to adjust to a perceived unpleasantry or hardship. Triumph over adversity in the great outdoors builds character and confidence that can be applied in every facet of one's life. Your state of mind can turn a negative situation around. Once, while alone in the high country, I found that I had no flashlight or candle to use at night. As my eyes became adjusted to the dark, I walked along the trail to a nearby overlook. Not only did the moon and stars illuminate the trail, but they also shone eerily down on the landscape below—a fantastic sight that I might have missed, had I sulked in camp wishing that I had a flashlight.

Hiking enthusiasts vary wildly in their methodologies. At one end of the spectrum are the "backpacking purists." They generally have the best gear and always are on the lookout for the latest of the outdoor outfitting industry's high-tech offerings. These folks' fare often consists of expensive freeze-dried food. Special fabrics and name-brand labels adorn their clothing. Cards, a radio, or any other diversions not directly related to the appreciation of nature are disdained. Always prepared and ready to help the ill-prepared, they rarely get in over their heads, saving the taxpayers dollars and the rangers headaches.

At the other end of the spectrum is the "make-do" backpacker, who can be spotted on the trail wearing too-tight jeans and some kind of camouflage shirt or hat. This type of individual probably borrowed half the equipment you see. A cheap oversized tent invariably announces these trekkers' presence. They will not hesitate to tote a cast-iron skillet to fry some bacon, and in camp they try to think of ways to use that big knife in the leather case attached to their belt. They are learning, and some eventually will move to a different place on the spectrum.

Between these groups are two others, the minimalists and the gearheads. Minimalists become obsessed with weight, paring their gear down to such a degree that their wilderness experience becomes a sheer survival test and much enjoyment is lost. I once stayed at a backcountry shelter with some hikers who drank hot water for breakfast; they felt that the pleasure of coffee did not justify its weight. Others become so concerned with pack weight that they cut off the ends of their toothbrushes to save a tenth of an ounce.

The gearheads, in contrast, have it all—and it is all in their pack. Around the fire you grumble about losing a tiny screw from your fishing reel, and ten minutes later the gearhead proudly returns with the exact size screw you needed. It is a good thing this type has a hot water bottle, because, after arriving late in camp, they need it to soothe the back muscles cramping from carrying all that extra equipment.

Pack weight always has been the subject of spirited mountaintop discussions. In general, beginning backpackers should carry no more than one-fourth their body weight and move up to a third of their body weight, if needed, as they become used to carrying a load. But wilderness adventuring has no commandments. No one is completely wrong, for all packers carry their own weight. While out there, I relish opportunities to see how others conduct business in the woods; I usually learn something, even if it is what not to do. Viewing my way as the only way merely restricts my growth.

I started out as a make-do backpacker. Ill-fitting secondhand combat boots, purchased at a local thrift store, adorned my feet. A twenty-dollar backpack with no padding on the shoulder straps carried hand-me-down gear, including a big knife. Nervously packing for my first solo overnight trip, I forgot to load my sleeping bag and spent all night wrapped in a green poncho while a screech owl's call pierced the dark, raising goosebumps on my skin. As time passed, I spent many dollars on faulty or unnecessary gear. I once bought a camp mirror and found out the hard way that I did not need or even want to see my own mug after three days in the forest. Personal appearance paled in interest, compared to towering trees and distant vistas.

I discovered that a positive frame of mind is of paramount importance. A poor state of mind is a poor piece of equipment. I try to be one with mountains and read their moods and adapt to whatever comes my way, using whatever resources I have available at the time. My mind is always there, and I rely on it as my most trusted piece of equipment.

Backpacking has health as well as aesthetic benefits. The ever-changing natural gymnasium exercises both mind and body. Weight watchers have a heyday, burning calories furiously on the trail. A nice climb makes clear the condition of lungs and heart, warning their owners to shape up. Legs get a thorough workout, toting body and gear. Setting up and operating in camp uses untold muscles in ways no machine can recreate. It is important that beginners not overtax themselves. As they hike more, distance and climbing abilities increase.

Human beings are incredibly resilient creatures. Today, however, far too often they look outside themselves for solutions to problems. My time in the woods has taught me to look inward in times of challenge and adversity. A long hike can be an opportunity for much-needed introspection.

In the outdoors, people today rely too much on technology. Can you imagine Daniel Boone's not exploring Kentucky because he had left his rain suit back in Tennessee? Even better role models are the mountaineers who settled the Smokies. Like them, I have developed a few unconventional practices, born of years of "testing" in the field. With all our petroleum-based equipment, we must not forget who we Americans are—people who persevered.

Over the years of changing seasons, for me life in the outdoors has evolved from a casual hobby to an all-consuming passion. That life has been both a refuge and a destination. Along the way I have accumulated many unforgettable experiences: watching the eyes of an old friend as she sees the sunrise from Mount Sterling for the first time, the camaraderie of new friends met around a toasty fire, the tug of a jumping rainbow trout on the end of a fishing line, sighting a secretive bear foraging for bugs in an old rotten log. These experiences cannot be bought; they can only be lived. I hope that the following stories of adventuring in the Smokies will inspire you to live some for yourself.

Acknowledgments

Usually a book has only one name beneath its title. This book, however, would not have been written but for many others to whom I am indebted. The book's very existence I owe to two dear old friends. Calvin Milam introduced this flatlander to backpacking and the Great Smoky Mountains. A sometime fellow backpacker, John Bland, and I used to recount mountain adventures in detail, and these conversations led me to keep a backpacking journal. After one particularly entertaining discussion, John, a professional editor, suggested that I write a book and offered his services as editor. The next thing I knew, I was writing the primitive version of *Trial by Trail*, which John helped to reshape into an improved version.

As the project grew, I needed help from others. I owe thanks to these special people: Ken Ashley, Debbie Daniels, Margaret Decker, Bryan Delay, Phyllis Henry, Ann Leeds, my mother Nelle Molloy, and Wes Shepherd. Special thanks go to Keith Horne for helping me through computer hell and to Meredith Morris-Babb for helping me see the book through to its end.

Summer

Don't Do It

Greenbriar to Newfound Gap

Our feet on a cliff, Calvin and I clung to loose, wet rocks. Through thick fog and billowing clouds, we could peer, intermittently, as far as thirty feet in front of us. I was drenched to the bone; the pack on my back felt like an anvil. In the ethereal beauty of the ragged, rocky landscape, we pondered what to do next. We had no idea where we were. Nor did we know our elevation; if we had, we might have been able to figure out where we were. Finally Calvin, his icy blue eyes visible through dripping blonde locks, looked at me and said, "There's only one way for us to go—up." This was my initiation into the world of wilderness travel.

It was proceeding terribly.

I had been the instigator of this misadventure. An epitome of the novice backpacker, I had made the classic mistake of biting off more than I could chew. In subsequent explorations of the Great Smoky Mountains, I have run into hundreds of beginners who, at home in the comfort of their easy chairs, looked at maps and thought they could march twelve or fifteen miles a day, usually with a grossly overloaded pack. Such aspiring hikers know they are heading into the mountains, but for some reason they do not register the fact that those twisting lines on the trail map go up and down in addition to north, south, east, and west. Ninety percent of the terrain in the Smokies has a grade of at least 10 percent.

Calvin and I, on our front porch back home in Knoxville,

had planned my initial backpacking trip. As I listened to his suggestions and experiences, my confidence mushroomed. I would climb those mountains as if they were anthills! I opened my big mouth and said, "Find the toughest hike in the book, and let's do it." The book in his hand was *Hikers Guide to the Smokies,* by Dick Murless and Constance Stallings.

So he found the Porter's Creek Trail, leading up to the Appalachian Trail (AT) and the Tennessee–North Carolina state line, in the Greenbriar section of the park, in Tennessee. The guide book states:

> For four miles it is an easy walking trail through the undisturbed forest. After that it turns into an unmaintained manway and becomes very steep, rising nearly 2,000 feet in the last mile. This section is for the experienced hiker only and even for him, one way. Nobody should attempt to descend this trail from the AT. The latter section is the most difficult and dangerous stretch of trail described in this entire guidebook. Don't do it!

Having read that, we had to do it.

The next day we gathered our gear and made the customary several stops between Knoxville and Gatlinburg to purchase fruit and stew meat and such odds and ends as water bottles, flashlights, and gourmet coffee. After arriving late at the end of Greenbriar Road and loading up, we hiked barely a mile before dusk. In the stifling summer humidity, our shirts were soaked. At the junction with the Brushy Mountain Trail, we set up camp in the dying June light just as a drizzly rain started. I had no idea at the time that we were getting off on the wrong foot by illegally camping at an undesignated site. I had entrusted the guiding duties to Calvin; this was my first trip. At this point, Calvin was not the most diligent follower of rules; he has grown since. We ended up eating snacks in the tent for supper, as the rain kept us from making a proper campfire. Now I am glad that we did not make one; we would have been breaking yet another park regulation: make fires only at designated campsites.

I tossed and turned that night, unaccustomed to sleeping on the ground and too excited about our challenge the next day.

First-time campers often have trouble sleeping in a wilderness setting. The dark of night and an overactive imagination mix, conjuring up wild animals, bad men, and other nebulous dangers. Hard ground and no pillow compound the problem.

Rain was still falling when I awoke; that dampened my spirits. I began to wonder if this was really a good idea after all. But Calvin was undaunted. We hurried through breakfast. After loading up, we donned our ponchos and packs and set off. The first two and a half miles were easy, as we trod uphill over a maintained trail. The mature forest formed a canopy that made morning seem like twilight, while Porter's Creek thundered down the valley floor beside the trail to our right.

At three and seven-tenths miles, at the Porter's Flat campsite, the maintained trail ended. We plowed on, discussing the trail description in the guidebook, which we had committed to memory. The rain came down in sheets, but we did not bother to stop, as the trail was marked with rock cairns—little piles of rock left by previous hikers to show the way. We proceeded along Porters Creek, fording it six times in half a mile. The rushing water ran no higher than our kneecaps on each crossing. I considered the possibility of a flash flood, though I noticed only a moderate rise in the creek. My real concern was finding the guiding rock cairns in the limited visibility of the summer thunderstorm.

Our ponchos soon were shredded from thrashing through the dense undergrowth along the creek. It did not matter, however, because each leaf, twig, and bush dumped a cargo of moisture on us as we swept past, soaking Calvin and me. We shed the ponchos and returned them to our packs. Our feet were wet from fording the creek. At that point, our trail was the creek itself. Here Calvin voiced his old adage, "Every trail bed is a creek bed."

The trail bed became steeper, but the rock cairns were still there to guide the way. Ahead, Calvin, attempting to lift himself onto a rock in the creekbed, slipped and smashed his shinbone, shedding blood and raising a painful knot. He shook off the pain and marched on. I admired his determination. We came to an open area marked by jumbled rocks. No cairns were

ASCENDING THE PORTER'S FLAT MANWAY. At that point, our trail was the
creek itself. Here Calvin voiced his old adage, "Every trailbed is a creekbed."

visible. Calvin backtracked, trying to find the last cairn we had seen, but to no avail. He returned, and at this point we agreed to stay together; to lose one another would make matters much worse. The two of us in vain searched the sloping mountainside for a marker. Even the immediate surroundings looked foreign. We now accepted the fact that we were lost. I began to wonder why I had ever wanted to do this. Fear enveloped me like the surrounding fog, which had swirled in behind us and settled. That fog blocked any hope of reorienting ourselves. We had not thought to bring a compass. At that point I vowed never to enter the woods without a compass. I have since broken that practical vow shamelessly. Of course the compass vow preceded by only moments my swearing off hiking altogether.

We headed straight up the steepest ragged gulch. That was another error. At that point a cairn marks a little opening in bushes to the left, and the real route swings around a steep rock outcrop and then heads up another ravine to Dry Sluice Gap and the AT. We struggled up the ravine hand over rock and finally settled, exhausted, on the godforsaken ledge. Grappling to surge upward, we had no real choice but to keep going up. Descending was even more dangerous than climbing.

I felt a wave of panic rising inside me; my voice quivered and cracked as I repeatedly apologized to Calvin for suggesting this hike as my initiation into the great outdoors. Luckily, just before I retched in my hysteria, Calvin reassured me that he could lead us on.

We continued upward, with Calvin in front. I crawled twenty-five feet but, due to the weight of my heavy pack, became dizzy and lost my balance. Suddenly I was falling—bounding, scraping, and sliding down the rock wall. Fruitlessly, I reached for handholds, tearing my skin, thumping the nerves in my paws. My feet flailed, searching for any impediment. I bounded like a rag doll down the rocky precipice. Enshrouded in fog, dampened by mist, my plunge took on the aura of an eerie slow-motion film. But my body was falling faster than my mind could comprehend. Suddenly, my descent stopped with a painful jerk, as I grasped a small outcropping of rock. My life-and-death grip endured, despite the wounds on my fingers and palms. I calmed myself and fought my way back up, gradually beginning to laugh and cry as Calvin, from above, urged me on. Having regained my position above the ledge, I collected my composure. We veered left into brush, then literally pulled ourselves upward while lying on our stomachs, gaining elevation all the while.

Now at almost five thousand feet, we alternately climbed, slithered, and crawled upward until, at last, we reached the top— the very peak of the ridge defining the state boundary between North Carolina and Tennessee. But the AT was nowhere to be seen. The fast-moving clouds soon parted, revealing the trail some two hundred feet below us. The death-defying climb we had just finished had been mostly in vain. But at least we knew where we stood. Knowing where you are after being lost is a great feeling!

We rested until our soaked bodies began to shiver and then hiked a mile or so west to Icewater Spring shelter, our original destination. There we were to rendezvous with friends. At the shelter, we changed into dry clothes and slipped into our sleeping bags. Although my hands, arms, and legs throbbed, I fell into a deep, luxurious sleep in the dry, dark shelter. After all the struggle, we had reached camp by one o'clock in the afternoon.

I awoke around seven that evening, hungry as a bear and feeling much better. The storm was long gone, having left a vivid, freshly washed sky in its wake. I sat outside the shelter breathing the clean air as Calvin tended my cuts with antiseptic cream from his small first-aid kit. He rustled up a supper of vegetable stew, while I convalesced.

Our pals arrived at sunset and we congregated at the fire, swapping tales. They could not believe our harrowing adventure. Next day we all hiked three happily uneventful miles along the AT to Newfound Gap, which was crowded with tourists enjoying the park from their automobiles. There were some vacationers from Ohio who had brought along their folding chairs, which they set out on the overlook.

I could not help but laugh as I compared their leisurely repose with the mountain hell Calvin and I had endured. What an initiation it had been!

Gimme Shelter

Pin Oak Gap to Laurel Gap

After ten-hour night shifts tending bar at a raucous campus saloon, veteran backpacker Bob Davis and I decided to rest up a while at Pin Oak Gap, our departure point, before we struck off on our adventure.

The gap is difficult to get to from my home base, Knoxville, Tennessee. Located on the winding Round Bottom Road on the North Carolina side of the Smokies, this spot marks the southern terminus of the Balsam Mountain Trail. We had crossed the Smokies via Newfound Gap Road in the night, turning onto the Blue Ridge Parkway and then back into the park on Balsam Mountain Road, which then turns into Round Bottom Road and passes through Pin Oak Gap.

Around 5:30 A.M., we arrived at the gap, pulled out our sleeping bags, and slept beside the truck. Bob woke me just before noon. I knew by looking at him that he was ready to hike. Below his droopy walrus mustache he wore a secretive smile, and his glasses were pushed to the back of his nose—the signal that he is ready to go.

The clear, crisp day signaled the arrival of autumn. The long hazy days of summer, when the sun heats the heavy, humid air, forming monstrous thunderheads, were just a memory in this neck of the woods. The cloudless cobalt blue sky afforded awesome mountain panoramas. It was simply a great day to hike. My new Vasque boots felt as comfortable as the re-

freshing breeze when I slid them on and prepared for the climb
of four and a half miles to Laurel Gap shelter.

Summer had peaked. The leaves on the trees would never
be greener, and, at five thousand feet, even the days would start
to cool soon. Half a mile beyond the truck, we left the old logging road upon which we were walking. Bob maintained his usual
snail's pace, stopping every now and then to wipe the moisture
from his glasses and then push them back on his nose. I tried
to hold back, but I was giving the new boots a run for their
money as Bob and I passed through a couple of dark and shady
hemlock stands to climb to Ledge Bald, now overgrown.

We continued down the trail, to arrive at Beech Gap, on
Balsam Mountain. During pre-park days, this was the location of
a logging camp. In fact, over 65 percent of the Smokies were harvested for timber. This particular spot has recovered well from its
scalping. Even the beech trees are back. They sometimes occur in
nearly pure stands in high, windy gaps. It is thought that they may
produce a chemical that discourages spruce and fir from growing in these gaps. These second-growth forests lack the splendor of virgin old-growth woods, but they are attractive in their
own right. The current beech trees may have survived the logger
but now face a new threat, an exotic bug known as the beech scale
insect. Less than half of the mature beech trees are left in New
England, where the beech scale insect has been active since the
turn of the century. Found in the Smokies in August 1993, the
trees of this park probably will suffer similarly. As of now, there is
no way to stop the bug, but some trees in the North are resisting
this European invader, offering hope for the future.

After resting among the beech trees, their smooth gray bark
cool on our backs, we slogged through a muddy section where my
new boots received their baptism in grime. On Balsam Hightop,
as I strolled among the Fraser firs there, my nose gloried in the
aroma of evergreens. Soon we arrived at the shelter. Around its
perimeter the fruits of summer abounded. Blueberries and blackberries hung heavy on the vine, even at this late date, August
30. An open, grassy area around the shelter revealed this spot
to be a bald that slowly was being reclaimed by the forest. The
origin of these balds near the tops of mountains is unclear; various
authorities believe they originated with fire, grazing, or Indians.

IN FRONT OF LAUREL GAP SHELTER. Despite my blisters, in such an idyllic setting, the sunny 65-degree weather made my spirits soar.

I settled near the shelter and took off my new boots, revealing a patchwork of nasty blisters on my feet. I had neglected the normal precaution of breaking them in before hiking because I had had an identical pair before these. And I had always felt that the boots actually break in the foot, rather than vice versa. My pair certainly was doing the job today. Despite my blisters, in such an idyllic setting as this, the mild, sunny weather made my spirits soar. I sat in the sun and read Johnny Majors' biography, *You Can Go Home Again*, while a cool mountain breeze tempered the warm air of the glade.

Then I walked barefoot among the brush, getting my fill of tasty pickings. Of the two fruits most plentiful in the Smokies, blueberries, with their dark sweet flavor, are my favorite. The tart and tangy blackberry, with its more watery texture, is a close second, but either berry can turn a bland pancake into a mountain morning delight.

Later I set up my hammock between two trees at the glade's edge and enjoyed a woodsy nap. Around 5 P.M., Bob began dinner and soon woke me to eat. Because the Laurel Gap shelter is one of the few in the park with a picnic table, his preparations were easier than usual. By the time we had set up and I had fetched water from the spring far down the hill from camp, it was dusk. We drank coffee with our ham and cheese sandwiches. After dining, we stored most of our gear and all of our food in the shelter. Our after-dinner cleanup was perfectly timed. Having just resettled around the table, we noticed the bear, on all fours, not ten feet from us. This bear was huge. He looked like he had been using the long daylight hours to fatten up for the cold winter. The abundance of berries and the prospect of human food at the shelter made this area part of his stomping grounds.

Many bears have figured out that the shelters along the AT inside the park can offer easy, delicious meals. Many backpackers ignore the posted signs warning against feeding bears. The creatures may appear cute and cuddly, but they are, of course, potentially dangerous wild animals. A wild animal is an unpredictable animal. Consequently many feeding incidents turn nasty.

Bears learn to associate backpacks with food. So they scare hikers into dropping their backpacks and then, with reckless abandon, go after the food inside. A bluff charge is their primary tactic for inducing fear. They stand on two legs and "woof," acting as if they are going to charge forward and attack. At this point it is hard to remember that the bear wants your food and not you. But it knows that you and your food must be separated. You must muster the courage to disregard the impulse to drop your pack and run nonstop to the car. Instead, face the bear. Eventually it will see that you are not going to fall for the bluff charge tactic and go away.

Never feed a bear, and never give up your equipment. If you do the latter, both you and the bear lose. You sacrifice your stuff, and the bear who encounters humans finds his life expectancy cut in half, according to research. Every instance in which his bluff charge is a success will encourage him to try it again on another backpacker.

You cannot blame bears for wanting human food. It is in their nature—they are opportunistic feeders, eating anything their territory offers them. When they emerge from their winter dens, pickings are slim. They survive on grasses and squawroot, which grows on the roots of oak trees. Then comes summer—the berry season. When the weather begins to cool, nuts and acorns become the main fare. In short, bears eat whatever is around, with 90 percent of that being plant matter. Ants, beetles, even carrion constitute part of their diet.

To promote a good time for all the creatures of the forest, including man, the three-sided stone shelters are fronted by chain-link fence and a latching gate. We were grateful for the shelter's presence, as the proper procedures for encounters with bears quickly flooded into and out of my mind. It was a lot easier to remember what to do when telling bear stories in the rec room back home.

The bear circled the camp perimeter, sniffing and huffing. We followed his moves in the dusky dark but had not yet sought out the shelter, the entrance to which lay about ten feet behind us. The bear passed back and forth in front of us, as we sat frozen at the picnic table. Having approached to within six or eight feet, the bear grew bored and disappeared. We quickly retreated to the shelter for the night, repeatedly commenting on the size of the bear, the likes of which I have not seen to this day.

We woke as early morning rays brightened the east-facing shelter. Shortly I hobbled outside barefoot, sipping coffee as the sun dried the morning dew and warmed the day to fifty degrees. My blistered feet still looked bad. After trying on the boots and stepping around the camp, I decided the discomfort was too great and the chances of further serious blistering too great. We would not hike on as originally planned.

The Park Service allows hikers only one night per shelter. But I felt that, under the circumstances, it would be worse to keep on hiking than to incur the wrath of the park ranger, who I hoped might understand after a look at my pus-covered feet.

It is best to wear your boots around town a lot before hitting the trail, so as to avoid a nasty blistering. Even so, walking around town is not hiking, so on the initial hike in new shoes you should bring moleskin along to cover a blister or hot spot and enable you to continue down the trail.

About 1 P.M., we were sitting around the table planning a luncheon feast. Since the bear sighting, we had been careful about what food we brought from the shelter and made sure to latch the gate behind us every time we left the structure. Bob's calm, quiet nature lent an air of serenity to the day. That sense of serenity, combined with the nearly perfect weather, led us to cook outside. Bears that are habituated to humans usually investigate a campsite around dusk and dawn, and this was midday. Bob heated up some corned-beef hash while I prepared the fixings. I laid out the paper plates and bread. As Bob spooned the hash onto the bread, one of my eyes focused on the greasy treat before us, while the other furtively glanced sideways and noticed the bear. Standing on hind legs at the glade's edge and guided by his keen nose, which he crinkled to the aroma of the hash, the bear slowly swiveled his giant head. This wild animal had proved his unpredictability by coming around at this time of day.

The evening before, we had noticed he was a big one, but on hind legs he looked positively frightening. His girth, under his shiny black coat, was that of a sumo wrestler. Muscles rippled as he moved. His eyes resembled those of that other eating machine, the shark. He moved our way; we snatched up the hot sandwiches and anything else we could get in an armload. We left the inedibles, including our stove, on the table.

With Bob right behind me, I scrambled into the shelter. I chained the gate shut just as the bear came up, rumbling and sniffing. He stood and shook the gate with his powerful arms, jerking it as much as slack would allow. I could see his sharp claws wrapped around the gate poles. We cowered in a dark corner, wondering what could be done. Of course, the answer was: nothing. Bob's usual calm had evaporated completely, increasing my already extreme agitation. In terror, we decided that if the bear got inside the shelter, we would dash out the gate as it came in.

Presently, the bear circled behind the shelter, out of our view. Deciding to strengthen our defenses, I used the opportunity to bolster the chained gate with some strong cord I had on hand. At about that time, the bear returned, rattling our cage

THE BEAR THAT TERRORIZED US. I chained the gate shut just as the bear came up, rumbling and sniffing. He stood and shook the gate with his powerful arms, jerking it as much as slack would allow.

for all it was worth. Bob and I exchanged looks of helpless panic.
The bear immediately ripped away my lashed cord as it if were
yarn. The two of us proceeded to gobble our food, nearly burning holes in our mouths, in hopes that the bruin would leave
once the aromatic edibles had disappeared.

As the bear persisted, Bob and I felt imprisoned in the shelter. From time to time the beast would wander around back of
the shelter or farther out into the campsite. We listened intently for sounds indicating his whereabouts. After a period of
silence lasting nearly an hour, we ventured outside the dark into
the warm and sunny day. No bear. We kept our eyes and ears
peeled for the forager throughout the afternoon, never relaxing
as we had the day before. By evening he had not returned, but
we decided against cooking anyway, not wanting to lure him
back.

About the time that he had shown up the night before, we
heard rustling in the brush. Our pulses jumped, and our hearts
raced. Though his efforts at getting our food so far had been
fruitless, save for scaring the socks off us, he was back! When
two hikers, a man and woman from coastal Carolina, emerged
from the trail, our chests sank in relief. Naturally, Bob and I
told the trekkers in vivid detail about our encounters with the
beast. Their mood seemed to change quickly from relief at reaching camp to wide-eyed apprehension.

Darkness fell as we four huddled in the asylum, waiting.
But the bear never returned. Our fellow woodlanders began to
wonder if we had put one over on them. Eventually we retired,
our comrades each keeping one eye open as they attempted to
sleep.

We awoke to a beautiful, crisp morning. Bob and I breakfasted inside the shelter. I faced the reality of hiking on blistered feet. Packing up, the two of us bid good luck to our ac-
quaintances and went our way, hobbling along with no bear in
sight.

Back on Rocky Top

Off-trail Hiking along Defeat Ridge, from Tremont to Spence Field

Wish that I was on ol' Rocky Top, down in the
    Tennessee hills;
Ain't no smoggy smoke on Rocky Top, ain't no
    telephone bills.
Once I had a girl on Rocky Top, half bear
    other half cat
Wild as a mink, but sweet as soda pop, I still
    dream about that.
Rocky Top, you'll always be home sweet
    home to me
Good ol' Rocky Top, Rocky Top, Tennessee;
    Rocky Top, Tennessee.

The University of Tennessee has a long and storied football tradition. Gridiron success has spawned a hyperloyal following
among alumni and natives of Tennessee—and I am both. As
one of the Big Orange faithful, I would do just about anything
to help the Volunteers win. With this in mind, I decided to
make a sojourn to a site within the Great Smoky Mountain
National Park that I associate with the Vols.

In the mid-1960s, Boudleaux Bryant and Felice Bryant wrote a country song inspired by the Smoky Mountains. Originally recorded by Archie Campbell but later duplicated by countless artists, "Rocky Top" evolved into the primary fight song for the Vols. "Rocky Top" also has become a nickname commonly used to designate UT's Shields-Watkins Field at Neyland Stadium, the university campus at Knoxville, and the city of Knoxville itself.

In the Smokies there is a place called Rocky Top. To enhance UT's chances of victory, I tried visiting this site at the beginning of the football season. After making two trips up there, followed by two years of Vol success on the field, I decided again to set out for Rocky Top, but this time with a variation.

A longtime hiking buddy, John Cox, agreed to go with me, despite some misgivings about the new route I had chosen. He saw that the trip portended catastrophe. John, large of frame, is not your stereotypical big man. Quiet and studious, he holds an engineering degree from the University of Tennessee. His inquisitive mind has stimulated many campfire reflections. He is always game for outdoor challenges, accepting any hardships that may come his way, so he was the ideal companion for this July outing.

The plan was to go to Rocky Top via Thunderhead Mountain, which lies .7 miles east of Rocky Top, along a well-marked path of the AT. But our task was getting to Thunderhead on the unmarked and unmaintained Defeat Ridge Manway. The only thing I knew then about this approach was that it started in Tremont and proceeded through a vast tract of remote, seldom-visited wilderness.

The path's namesake, Defeat Ridge—which in our case nearly lived up to its name—had always caught my eye when I inspected a map of the Smokies. The name originated in the 1830s, when those in power decided to build a toll road between Knoxville and the valley of the Little Tennessee River in North Carolina. A certain Isaac Anderson was in charge of building the Tennessee side of the road. In determining the exact route of the road through the Smokies, he enlisted the help of his Cherokee Indian work force. Each one indicated his choice with a vote; having no *V* in their language, however, they said "Bote." So the ridge they selected became Bote Mountain, and the ridge they did not choose, immediately east of Bote Mountain, became known as Defeat Ridge.

Preparing for the trip, John and I loaded our minimal provisions at the end of Tremont Road, where our expedition to Rocky Top was to begin. This point lies at the confluence of the Middle Prong of the Little River and Thunderhead Prong. In preparation for the trip, we had zealously pared our gear to the barest essentials, eliminating soap, books, extra clothes, and other dispensable articles. We also made appropriate substitutions—one small pot in lieu of a cooking kit, a candle rather than a Coleman lantern, and so on. I even cut the width and length of my closed-cell foam sleeping pad, to diminish snagging on foliage and to reduce weight.

We first had obtained an off-trail permit to camp overnight in an undesignated site. When obtaining a permit—which is done through a park ranger, usually in person—you must state your approximate expected overnight location. Getting such a permit was a good idea, because if we became lost, the rangers would have somewhere to start looking for us.

In the Great Smoky Mountains National Park, "off-trail" is a vague term. Long before the park was established, humans occupied the land. The first white settlers, arriving around the beginning of the nineteenth century, set up simple farms. The early settlers and later their descendants built roads and trails to meet their needs. Many of these thoroughfares followed paths established by the Cherokee Indians, who themselves had built upon game trails worn by the true trailblazers—wild animals who occupied the land before any humans, white or otherwise, appeared.

Later came the loggers, who cleared and graded great swaths through the mountains for their logging operations. More than fifty years have passed since the last organized logging outfits left. But their imprints still can be seen today, if one looks closely. In the days shortly after the establishment of the national park, the federal Civilian Conservation Corps (CCC) improved old trails and created new ones through the park. For lack of funds for maintenance, many of these have been lost to the forest. The result is a myriad of unmaintained trails, ranging from totally overgrown and impossible to find or follow, to trails rivaling the maintained ones but kept up by fishermen, horse riders, and other outdoors people. An off-trail enthusiast can enjoy many of these unmaintained park trails.

Our chosen route was an old railroad grade that the CCC had turned into a trail. Our late 5 P.M. start, however, necessitated a strategy of getting off in the right direction; finding the old railroad grade, which we hoped to follow along the lower reaches of Thunderhead Prong; and then, at a campsite along the prong, resting up for an anticipated grueling climb the next day. Having loaded up, we departed in a sliver of summer sunlight. After crossing the Little River on a wooden plank bridge, we veered right and immediately spotted the old railroad grade. Human traces are easily identified by the experienced eye, as no straight lines or flat, squared-off spots exist in nature. The actual rails had been removed, but other railroad remnants included lumps of coal and evenly spaced, now-rotten railroad ties.

Within a hundred feet of the outset, we had to cross Thunderhead Prong, which we accomplished by rock-hopping over slick, moss-covered stones. John and I ambled easily along the creek, where fishermen had cleared some of the bank. But about half a mile up, after another creek crossing, the anglers' trail petered out.

Nowadays, a strangely out-of-place wooden sign proclaims that the area currently is closed to maintain a human-free habitat for the reintroduced red wolf. Absent from the hills of East Tennessee since the beginning of the twentieth century, reintroduction of this carnivore was a first for a national park. The Smokies were chosen because they comprise a large protected land area. Wild animals, however, cannot understand the concept of a protected boundary. So, with the initial test reintroduction of four red wolves in the park in late 1991, the animals were fitted with radio collars that enable researchers to track their movements. There was some straying from the park and killing of farm animals, but the owners were recompensed in kind for their losses. Overall, park biologists felt that the test was successful.

A year later, two separate families—each consisting of an adult male, an adult female, and their four offspring—were released. One family was released in the Cades Cove area, and another in the Tremont area. The results have been mixed. The family released into Cades Cove displaced the coyotes that had migrated back into the park in the early 1980s. A litter of four pups was born in the wild, but all contracted a parvovirus and died. Three other pups were born of the Tremont family; one fell prey to coyotes, one left the park and is in an acclimation pen, and the other was moving freely outside the park.

Other wolves, introduced to the park as adults, also have had mixed results. As of December 1994, six are still free in the park. The Cades Cove group was recaptured after preying on newborn calves in the cove. A solar-powered electric holding pen is scheduled to be built to protect the calves until they are ten days old. The Cades Cove group then will be rereleased.

According to wildlife biologist Kim DeLozier, more releases are scheduled in other areas of the park. It had been hoped that the park eventually could support a population of fifty wolves, but that figure has been revised downward. The current estimate is that a total of one hundred of these animals may be roaming the Southern Appalachian Mountains. Even so, DeLozier believes that the red wolf is here to stay.

As John and I continued our journey, I spotted the railroad grade turning left, moving up and away from the creek, through an open hardwood forest interspersed with stands of hemlock. We began to follow it upward, sweat tumbling down our foreheads. The air, thick with moisture, seemed to impede our progress. The deep green vegetation looked as if the leaves were sweating, too. Water gathered on the low-slung tips of ferns. The saturated ground further attested to the fact that the area had been wracked by a thunderstorm earlier that day. All this made for wet trekking.

The grade now led far from the creek, and I became concerned about where it led. So we stopped our sweaty march for a map consultation. A methodical, then frantic, search through my pack yielded no map. I had left it either in the Jeep or at

home. Either way, I was going to go on stubbornly without it—
an unwise proposition. Putting on an air of confidence, I attempted to assure John that we would not get lost. But it was
easy to read the uncertainty in his eyes. The word *fiasco* kept
flashing in my brain.

We went back down to the creek and found our way through
the dense vegetation that typically flourishes along creeks in the
Smokies. With continual scanning, I spotted the railroad grade up
on the hill to our left, and we scrambled up the steep wooded hill
once again to follow the grade. It had deviated away from the
creek, only to switch back and parallel the creek again, but without a map I had not known. At this point, the grade was easy to
follow (it seemed particularly easy after fighting our way along the
rhododendron-choked creek), though fern and brush ground
cover and many small trees were reclaiming the path. The sky
was darkening, so we began to look for a campsite.

John found a fairly flat spot in a gloomy hemlock thicket
alongside Thunderhead Prong. We laid our packs against a wet
log rotting rapidly in this dim, damp forest. I slid steeply down
to the prong and cooled my sweat-soaked body in the mountain water. Then I changed into dry clothes and began to set
up camp. John constructed a fire ring of surrounding stones and
gathered downed wood while I fetched water from the creek
and organized our food for the night.

We ate tortilla chips and salsa dip as an appetizer as we
read that day's Knoxville newspaper, using some sections to
kindle the fire. John served up rare steak sandwiches on large
onion rolls, topped with thick slabs of summer tomatoes and
sweet Vidalia onions, complemented by fresh corn, cut from
the cob and sautéed in butter. Oddly, the sky became lighter
just before night came on, as a rack of clouds scudded past our
camp. Later, we found it hard to stay awake in the dim candlelit
evening, so we soon fell asleep.

I woke at daylight to find a slight chill in the upland air.
As I brewed coffee on my Svea stove, the pungent aroma awakened John. We hastily breakfasted on spicy hot sausage, rolls,
and corn grits, while anticipating a big day. Corn was a staple
of the hill people's diet a century ago and was figuring promi-

nently in ours. At 8:30, we left our now traceless campsite after reclothing ourselves in still sweat-soaked hiking duds. We scrambled back to begin tracing the railroad grade as it continued its steady ascent. The journey went well until we encountered our first briar thicket. We faced a dilemma. If we went around it, we had steep slopes to climb, as well as possibly losing the grade. But if we forged through the briars, we were sure to get scratched up, in our shorts and T-shirts. Here is where I learned a lesson: in hiking off-trail, always wear long garments. We slowly picked our way through the briar patch, prying apart the thorny arms of the bushes and scarfing down tasty blackberries, a peace offering from the gnarly greenery.

We headed north to the crest of the loftiest mountains in the East.

A scant hundred yards later, we hit another thicket. But this one was different from the thicket before—it looked as if it had been trampled down. Then we noticed the bear scat; a bear had been here recently, eating its share of berries. Bears are creatures of habit, and they were keeping the track partially open as a well-used game trail. The thick fur of a bear is quite adequate defense against the sharp needles of a briar thicket. In the next mile, we passed around and through some twenty thickets. Long bright red scratches adorned our arms and legs. Seed-laden bear scat covered the ground and stuck to our boot soles. Finally the hollow mercifully narrowed and the grade, in consequence, ran closer to the creek, among thick but not prickly rhododendron.

Suddenly the grade tacked to the right, to cross Thunderhead Prong. The rotting remnants of an old wood railroad bridge looked oddly out of place in this ancient wilderness. By rock-hopping, we crossed the rivulet at an elevation of thirty-two hundred feet.

While crossing the watercourse, I kicked over a rock at the water's edge, and a dark salamander skittered for cover. I picked it up before it could find shelter. Its response was to bite the tip of my index finger. Rather hurriedly I set it back down to join its comrades, who in the Smoky Mountains reach their greatest numbers for a temperate climate. Biting is not the only defense mechanism these amphibians use. They also sacrifice their

JOHN COX CROSSING THUNDERHEAD PRONG. We crossed the now-small
rivulet, at an elevation of 3,200 feet, by rock-hopping.

tails to predators and simply grow another tail to replace one
lost. Some have toxic skin. If the toxicity is not effective, they
will play dead. Sometimes a nontoxic salamander will fool its
enemies by looking like a toxic one. Usually they combine one
or more of these techniques. Although insects are their pre-
ferred fare, they often prey upon their own kind.

But these are mere generalities; it would take a whole book
to describe each of the more than twenty-five species of salamanders that inhabit the park from one end to the other, living
under logs, in the water, and anywhere else that is moist and dark.
Probably the most peculiar and certainly the largest salamander is
the hellbender. Living in streams in the park lowlands, they can
reach two or more feet in length! Being so strange and ugly, they
used to be killed upon sight, but no longer. Part of the mosaic of
life in the Smokies, they do a little killing of their own. Min-

nows, worms, crawdads, and small fish are their prey. Salamanders are a prime example of just how fertile the Smokies are.

Twenty minutes after a water break, John and I resumed our climb out of the Thunderhead Prong watershed and up the side of Defeat Ridge. Our progress was slow but steady. We knew which way to go, as the grade could be followed, but the mountain laurel, rhododendron, and other vegetation slowed us down. At times the thickets were so dense that I was reminded of movie actors hacking their way through a remote South American jungle.

Around noon, we gained the top of the ridge at a confusing switchback, where the trail seemingly died in a "hell." That is the name old-timers gave large growths of rhododendron, because of the difficulty of getting through them. I tore my way around in circles, tripping over crowded reddish-brown limbs contrasting with waxy dark green leaves, until finally I picked up the trail. John and I were elated, thinking that the ridge top would be easier going. We were very much mistaken in that assumption, however.

At four thousand feet, the railroad grade turned west off Defeat Ridge, eventually to connect with Bote Mountain. A nearby hemlock tree was used as a territory marker by the local bruins, for I observed their telltale scratches in the bark, usually at or above the five-foot mark, and the coarse black hair caught in the splintered wood. This was further evidence that bears often used this trail. We stayed the course, moving northward up the ridge, while the thickets became more overgrown than ever. Repeatedly John and I had to get down on our hands and knees and crawl on wet, dead leaves through the long and appropriately named hells, our packs constantly catching on branches. How happy we had been earlier, when we achieved the ridge top. Now we were exhausted, wearing a coat of sweaty dirt and with no end of punishment in sight.

Three merciless hours later, soiled, wet, thirsty, and generally beaten down, we came to a spring. Now I felt confident that we were high on Thunderhead Mountain. I had heard talk of a spring just below the summit of the mountain on its Tennessee side. We drank our fill of the cool mountain water, while

a dense fog shrouded the mossy mountainside. It was difficult
to get going again, but at fifty-five degrees, our wet, tired bodies began to chill, forcing us to move on or get colder. It was
hard to believe how hot we had been a day earlier, at the lower
elevations.

Twenty minutes later, I noticed light brightening on the
south side of the forest. Suddenly I burst into a wet, foggy field
of grass—Thunderhead! I whooped and hollered in celebration.
Despite his bedraggled appearance, John could not have looked
happier had he won the lottery. It had taken us over eight hours
to go an estimated five miles, gaining thirty-five hundred feet.
We made the last hundred feet to the top of Thunderhead,
dropped our packs, and changed into clean, dry clothing. We
celebrated with coffee and apples.

It was now 6 P.M. We forced our aching bodies into motion for the three-quarter-mile hike to Rocky Top. We couldn't
see it from Thunderhead; due to the fog, we couldn't see even
twenty feet in front of us. All that hard work, not to be rewarded with a view! Finally we arrived at Rocky Top, battered
and ready to drop. We rested again and took a few photos as
proof of our presence. Then I stepped on the highest rock and
said my prayer for the Vols.

I felt much better about the upcoming football season, but
not the upcoming days ahead, knowing how sore I would be.
Tired as we were, we had to move on to Spence Field, where
we would camp at the shelter. There a throng of children and
parents awaited us, and we were none too pleased to see them.
So we filed on to another site nearby, where we could relax until bedtime, when we would retire to the shelter.

I brewed coffee as we discussed our march. Then I heard a
rustle in the brush behind me. A female black bear with a cub
at her side stared at us from a distance of not more than ten
feet. My initial emotion was anger, for I was far too exhausted
to deal with the situation. I swung around and faced the bear,
banging my small pot with its lid. The cub scrambled up to
safety in a nearby tree. The big bear huffed and puffed, display-
ing its teeth and making false charges. We held our ground.
We had made too much effort to get here to be run off by a

bear, though actually we were in its domain. The bear realized that we were not going to part with our food, so she and her cub filed off into a wooded hillock.

Immediately the two of us decided to make ourselves less attractive to the bear by eating our food. We started eating, keeping our eyes peeled for the bear. Suddenly John yelled. The she-bear had pulled an end-around on us and positioned herself downwind of our food. Her nose scanned the air, perhaps to see if she liked what we were eating. John started chewing faster, looking rather comical as he stuffed a bagel slathered with cream cheese into his already full mouth. The bear made a bluff charge again, which we rejected, staring at her face until she rumbled off into the steep woodlands.

We moved yet again that day, to a high point on Spence Field, and watched the sun set. As night arrived, we returned to the shelter beneath a starry sky. At the shelter, John and I quietly crept in, spread our bedrolls, and fell into the deepest sleep.

It was a tough task getting my aching body out of my cozy sleeping bag the next morning, but we wanted to see the sunrise. As if just for us, the morning sun rose over an imposing Thunderhead Mountain. After a quick morning repast, we were off the sunny bald and down into the woods. The two of us descended the old road born of Cherokee labor, the Bote Mountain Trail. It was six miles of sore-legged walking to the Jeep. But the off-trail hike was a success, and the Vols were gonna win!

Fall

Tramping through the High Country

Newfound Gap to Round Bottom

The AT is the longest continuously marked footpath in the world. Many people attempt to hike its entire length of two thousand miles, but only a hundred or so each year make it all the way. Most hikers enjoy the AT in much shorter segments. A 68-mile segment forms the backbone of the 850-mile Great Smoky Mountains Trail System, much of which also marks part of the state line between North Carolina and Tennessee. In fact, the main crest of the Smokies is often referred to as Stateline Ridge.

John Cox and I chose a route along this boundary trail as part of a two-night backpacking trip. It was a rainy morning late in October when we set out for Newfound Gap in the heart of the Smokies.

Newfound Gap (elevation 5,040 feet) is an important location in the park. The road bisecting the Smokies goes through the gap and is named for it. United States President Franklin Delano Roosevelt dedicated the national park here in 1940. In the park, the gap serves as the central trailhead for the AT, which extends east for thirty-one miles and west for thirty-seven before leaving the park's confines. The AT comprises less than 10 percent of the park's trail mileage, but it carries well over half of all hikers. This traffic makes the AT busy and well-trodden, especially near Newfound Gap and Clingman's Dome.

John and I were heading east and had the trail to ourselves. We were attempting to traverse all the trails within the park, and we also wanted to learn more about the spruce-fir forest community that dominates the highest ridges of the Smokies. Our continual ascent went slowly while we adjusted to our heavy packs. Although the temperature, at sixty degrees, was relatively warm, mist draped the spruce-fir forest and slowly saturated us. When the forest is fogged in, it is difficult to gauge distance, and you never know how far you have traveled. But we were not in a rush.

Each time I enter the spruce-fir forest, especially when it fogged in (and it often is), I am stunned at how much it differs from the forests of the nearby lowlands. The flora is unlike that anywhere else in Dixie. Although this forest comprises only 2 percent of the park's land area, it is a major reason for the park's protected status.

The very existence of this southernmost stretch of spruce-fir forest is being threatened. The red spruce, one of the high-country forest community's two major trees, was heavily logged during World War I for use in constructing airplanes. This tree is faring decently now, though acid rain may be slowing growth rates. The other tree, the Fraser fir, is being attacked by an exotic invader, an insect called the woolly adelgid. In the United States, since the turn of the century, the insect has made its way south from Maine, having arrived in the Smokies in 1963. Within ten years all the fir stands in the park were affected. As small as the creatures are, their handiwork is highly visible; gray remains of firs that have shed their needles can be seen along the AT between Clingman's Dome and Mount Guyot.

About a mile and a half from the trailhead, at six thousand feet, we reached Mount Kephart and the Sweat Heifer Trail junction, where the Fraser firs grow in nearly pure stands. But, if infested, they can die in a decade. The Sweat Heifer Trail descends into North Carolina, but we pushed forward on the AT through fading mist for another mile, to the Boulevard Trail junction.

At this junction, John and I dropped our packs for a little side trip. About seventy-five yards down the Boulevard Trail, we took a narrow side trail for half a mile among the spruce to a steep precipice appropriately named Jump Off. We looked out. Ominous clouds hung low in the surrounding valleys and blew past so closely overhead that it seemed we could touch their dark, moisture-laden bottoms. Just below, across the deep valley of Porter's Creek, rocky Charlie's Bunion stood out on the forest-cloaked Stateline Ridge. The dead gray trunks of the firs contrasted with the living greenery on the sides of Mount Chapman and Mount Guyot to the east. Charlie's Bunion was treeless, too, but for another reason. In 1925, fire had ravaged a four-hundred-acre section of Stateline Ridge, killing the plant life that survived on the thin layer of soil covering the rocky backbone of the crest. With no living root structure to hold the soil in place, heavy rains four years later resulted in a massive slide, revealing the rock outcrop visible today.

Returning to our packs, we moved on, passing the overused (and now closed) Icewater Spring shelter. The spring for which it is named is one of the Smokies' finest. John and I stopped for a drink, then began the mile-long, five-hundred-foot descent to Charlie's Bunion, our proposed lunch site. We picked our way carefully on the wet, stony trail.

At the Bunion, John dropped his pack, noting the absence of other hikers at this popular day hike destination with the catchy name. Writer Horace Kephart had played a hand in Smoky Mountain lore here as elsewhere. After the big mudslide that exposed the outcrop in 1929, Kephart and some of his cronies, including one Charlie Conner, went to examine the site. While there, Conner took off his shoe to check a foot ailment. On the spot, Kephart thought up the new name for the location and subsequently had it put on official maps of the Smokies.

The weather was working in our favor; there were no soil-loosening storms about. The mist had evaporated, allowing us a dry lunch and a great view. Many believe that Charlie's Bunion has the best views in the park. It makes you realize just how high you are in the mountains. Sharp cliffs drop off into Greenbriar Valley below. To the west, prominent Mount LeConte stands tall in its majesty. The view into Tennessee extends as far as the clarity of the sky allows. But this steep area can be dangerous, too. A few years ago, a teenage boy on a day hike with his church group slipped off the narrow trail and fell to his death.

Out of my pack I pulled turkey-and-cheddar sandwiches I had made at home. The steady wind made the only sound on this dark day, as we ate and watched the clouds scuttling by. Fall's brief colors tinted nearby Greenbriar Pinnacle and the valleys and ridges below. The deciduous trees were bare only at their highest points.

Soon we resumed our hike, passing the Richland Mountain Trail junction and entering an area known as the Sawteeth. From afar, as a result of the same 1925 fire that spawned Charlie's Bunion, this area looks jagged. The rocky ridge is very narrow here—in some places ten feet or less—but offers views into North Carolina and Tennessee. Past False Gap, the former location of an AT shelter, we began climbing. We had traveled six miles from Newfound Gap.

On down the trail, a sign indicated that we were at Laurel Top. But there was no view, and we were not on top of anything, so far as I could see. Those who named the location must have been higher up the ridge. John and I pressed on. I kept thinking about the future of the forest we were in. The woolly adelgid has no natural enemies in this country, but young firs are less susceptible to them. Pesticides work but are too harmful to the rest of the ecosystem. The Park Service does use one insecticide soap that is less damaging, but it requires intensive spraying from a truck. This limits its use to areas along Clingman's Dome Road, leaving vast stretches of forest to the bug that already has killed 90 percent of the mature Fraser firs. And since all elements of an ecosystem are tied together, as one element goes, so go the others. The primary foods for two birds, the red crossbill and the red-breasted nuthatch, are the seeds of the red spruce and the Fraser fir. The Smoky Mountains are these birds' most southern range. What will happen to them when half their food supply is gone? Perhaps the young trees can keep producing seedlings before they are killed off, perpetuating the tree despite the woolly adelgid.

Finally, after ten miles on the AT, we reached Peck's Corner shelter, located half a mile down the Hughes Ridge Trail.

EAST TENNESSEE FROM THE SAWTEETH. The rocky ridge here is very narrow—at some points ten feet or less—but it offers views into North Carolina and Tennessee.

A drizzle began as we eagerly headed down to the shelter, hoping to have it to ourselves. But smoke emanating from the shelter chimney told us that it was already occupied. We were disconsolate. Inside the shelter, two fifty-year-old men had their gear spread out all over the place. As we stood there wondering what to do, a group of teenage Floridians noisily approached. We decided to brave the elements and camp in a small gap just above the shelter. It was now 5 P.M.

Setting our packs down felt good after the long first day. John set up a piece of plastic as a windbreak, helping to abate the draft, as I brewed a warm pot of coffee. Deciding to gamble that the drizzle would be brief, we confirmed the decision to stay outside rather than in the shelter with a group of unknowns.

Now, I am glad shelters are there. They have helped me to brave the weather and provided refuge on many a harsh highland night. I have met and learned from many interesting people at these shelters. But friends and I go camping together because we enjoy sharing the solitude and camaraderie with each other, not necessarily with other hikers. At backcountry campsites, we may be in the same general area as other campers but can maintain a polite distance, interacting at will and then returning to our respective camping areas. Shelters are quite another story, however. Shelters have either six or seven double bunks, each with a bed down low and another above. The bunks are located right beside each other, all in an area approximately fifteen by twenty feet. When each backpacker's equipment is added, the shelter can become very overcrowded.

In such a cramped setting, different backpacking styles sometimes give rise to conflict. I have seen litterbugs leave a mess, "lumberjacks" cut down live trees for firewood, and others exercise utter lack of consideration for their fellow shelter occupants. I do not come to the mountains to play forest cop, so usually I am not inclined to set uninformed hikers straight. I am not perfect myself, and I do not want to lecture people I don't even know. But I hate to see uncaring individuals come in and damage an area that means so much to me—one that, as Americans, we all are responsible for. So, if a conflict arises, I assess each situation individually. And I usually hike in the less heavily traveled areas of the park.

It was time for supper and time to light my lantern. I chopped stew meat into two cans of pork and beans and heated them in a pot on my stove. As we had no campfire, the meal warmed us up. I knew the real chill would come when the clouds departed, as they were predicted to do, and the "warm" air could escape. It was just above fifty degrees. We lay in our bags and read until about nine o'clock, then ended our evening early.

The morning dawned sunny and cool. Just as predicted, the clouds had dispersed during the night, and the temperature had dropped. At 8 A.M., it was now thirty-eight degrees. The night before, I had placed my stove close to me, so that I could light it and place a pot of water on it without leaving my sleeping bag. Before I knew it, the water was boiling, forcing me to get up. The coffee I made warmed me from inside out. "Baghdad"

DEATH ON MOUNT CHAPMAN. The many dead trees attest to the troubles facing these forests.

John, nicknamed for his reluctance to emerge from his sleeping bag in the morning, was holding out for the sun to warm the day. But the smell of link sausage frying in the pan got him stirring. I then mixed half a dozen eggs with some Half-and-Half I had brought in little restaurant-sized packets, and scrambled the mixture in the sausage grease. We ate, using bagels to sop up any grease remaining on our paper plates. John and I then packed up, leaving Peck's Corner around 9:30.

We continued northeast on the AT. In two and a half miles we crossed over Mount Sequoyah, named for the Tennessee-born Indian who created the Cherokee alphabet. Just past Chapman Gap, we began climbing Mount Chapman, again achieving an elevation of six thousand feet. The many dead trees we encountered on Mount Chapman testified to the troubles these forests face. Besides the woolly adelgid, air pollution constituents such as ozone are thought to be damaging life in the high country. Surprisingly, among areas in the United States, the Smokies rank second, behind the Los Angeles Basin, in stagnant air occurrences. As a result, ozone is thought to be affecting up to ninety of the park's plant species, while visibility from peaks in the Smokies, especially in the summer months when air stagnation most often occurs, simultaneously is declining.

Another possible source of damage to park flora is acid rain. Some parts of the Smokies receive ninety inches of precipitation annually, and many experts believe that elements of this rain are harmful. The frequent fog and cloud cover in the high country make it even more susceptible. The effects of acid deposition on the environment are very complicated to study. Acid infiltrates soils and streams, so its action defies quantification. No effects of acid rain have been shown to be helpful to the environment, however.

From Mount Chapman, the view of nearby Mount Guyot (at 6,621 feet the second highest peak in the Smokies) revealed large areas of gray, dead tree trunks—yet more evidence of the serious problems facing the Park Service. Nowadays the gray expanse of death on the west side of Guyot is one of its identifying features. We made the sharp, short descent down Mount Chapman to Big Cove Gap and then climbed to the Tricorner Knob shelter (elevation 5,920 feet). There we decided to rest.

It was 11:30 A.M., sunny and fifty degrees. The golden fall sun warmed my body as I escaped the troubles of the high country. John whipped up a prepackaged macaroni salad. After lunch we lay about until 1:30. I took a short walk, seeing the lush undergrowth of ferns at this elevation, as well as the carpet of the spruce-fir forest, known as club moss, which is in the fern family. Spongy and bright green, the club moss looks almost fake. Highlanders at the turn of the century used to gather and sell it for hard cash for its use in making flash photographs.

A short way beyond the shelter was our turn off the AT, onto the Balsam Mountain Trail. It is one of the nicest trails in the Smokies. Relatively flat for a mountain trail, lightly traveled, it stays above five thousand feet for eight and a half miles, traversing spruce-fir country. But we planned to follow it just four-tenths of a mile to the closed Hyatt Ridge trail. We found the old overgrown trail and began following it south. In a short time, however, we encountered a series of briar thickets and felled trees that quickly discouraged us. We were off-trail green-horns and for once wisely decided to turn back.

Within minutes we were again on the Balsam Mountain Trail, wondering what to do. Our permit stated that we were going to the McGhee Spring campsite, which we would have reached had our off-trail venture succeeded. But it was fourteen miles away by maintained trail, and the hour was 2 P.M., too late to set out. After encountering the crowd at Peck's Corner, we were leery of staying at Tricorner Knob, so we decided to go to Laurel Gap, a shelter but one off the AT. We marched southeast on the gently undulating Balsam Mountain Trail over Thermo Knob, reaching six thousand feet again as we hiked on around the south side of Luftee Knob. Four miles from Tricorner Knob, we passed the top end of the Gunter Fork Trail. Trees other than the evergreens had adapted to the harsh climate, we noticed. Mountain ash, beech, and yellow birch provided a deciduous complement for the forest. In less than two hours, we had walked over six miles, passing the Mount Sterling Ridge Trail just before the descending two hundred yards to the Laurel Gap shelter. We arrived about 4 P.M.

John broke out the snacks while I went to get water. We refueled with dried banana chips, oatmeal creme pies, and pretzel sticks. I enjoyed the last of the warm sun.

One strange item unique to the Smokies highlands is the summer-blooming Rugel's ragwort, whose flowers have a scent resembling that of a skunk. The Park Service maintains a close eye on its extremely limited habitat. The death of the firs may be diminishing the places where it grows. Another unusual plant is the aven, with one population on Mount LeConte. Ironically, because of their rarity, such unusual plants sometimes fall prey to unscrupulous plant collectors.

I checked the shelter. Two sleeping bags and gear were laid out on the top bunks, but the owners were not around. We would have company for the evening. After dusk, the air cooled quickly. As we built our fire at the shelter hearth, our two fellow hikers showed up. They were two students from the University of Georgia. Their sleeping bags looked awfully flimsy, and the temperature was already below forty degrees. They were in for a cold night.

We all sat around the fireplace under my bright lantern, changing places periodically to share the heat from the fire. I cooked up a box of Suzi Wan Chinese food, into which I mixed some canned chicken. It tasted good, but we could have eaten more. John and I stayed up until ten, then spread our sleeping bags outside in the open glade by the shelter and quickly fell asleep under the starry sky.

When we awoke to a cloudy dawn, the temperature hovered just above freezing. I immediately made us cups of hot chocolate, which we drank as we packed our gear. Hot chocolate is a good choice for a quick-start breakfast because it makes you feel full for a little while and is faster than cooking breakfast. John led the way as we hiked southwest over Balsam High Top, then two miles down to Beech Gap. The crisp air was ideal for walking; only my fingertips were chilled. At Beech Gap, we began a steady descent on the Beech Gap Trail to Round Bottom Horse Camp, dropping below five thousand feet for the first time since we left Newfound Gap. Leaving the high country behind, we blazed down the trail with our light packs. Three miles later we were at the Straight Fork Road.

Since our off-trail attempt had been thwarted, we were thirty or more auto miles from the Jeep. Luckily, our Georgian shelter mates had promised us a ride to Newfound Gap Road. They showed up an hour behind us, and we all piled into a small economy car. They dropped us off at Newfound Gap Road, and we hitched a cold ride in the bed of a Chevy pickup back up to Newfound Gap. Around noon we were back at the Jeep, with more knowledge and trail mileage in the Smokies under our belts.

Looping the Loop

Up and Down around Cades Cove

The swiftest traveler is he who goes afoot.
—Henry David Thoreau

As I approached the Cooper Road trailhead, the autumn sun slipped behind gathering clouds, drawing my attention to the weather. Having just left the Abrams Creek ranger station, I was embarking upon a five-night solo circuit around the perimeter of Cades Cove, located in the northwestern corner of the Great Smoky Mountains National Park.

According to weather reports, rain was likely, but I was not too concerned, as this was October, historically one of the least rainy months in the Smokies. I figured that any rainy spell would be relatively brief. A warm, blustery wind blew early fall leaves across the road-turned-trail. One of the earliest routes into mountain-rimmed Cades Cove, Cooper Road leads to the large, open valley cleared and settled in the early 1800s. Now many of those buildings erected by the Cades Cove pioneers have been preserved. A popular eleven-mile road loops around the cove, passing many of these former homesteads. Hiking and horse trails extend from this road to connect with other trails in the park.

With the towering hemlocks a mile behind me and the rocky crossing of Kingfisher Creek half a mile back, I left the Cooper Road Trail, then turned east on the much narrower

Little Bottoms Trail. A relatively new trail constructed in the 1960s following an older settlers' path, it passes over a steep, short ridge to enter the valley of Abrams Creek. As I topped the ridge, the rumble of a mile of Abrams rapids filled my ears. Hearing this, I shot haphazardly down the trail, so excited by the prospect of autumn trout fishing that I gave no thought to the trees crowding the thin trail so closely that their spidery roots reached up to become stumbling blocks. I visualized myself standing in the rushing creek, rod bent, reeling in a hard-fighting rainbow, the action framed in the wooded setting of fall's peaking golds, reds, and yellows.

At this time of year, the first heavy frosts paint the forests in brilliant colors. Actually, at this twelve-hundred-foot elevation, the leaves were only beginning to change, though the sourwoods already showed off reddish-purple leaves. Overall, it is difficult to pinpoint the peak leaf coloration time in the Smokies. First, different types of trees turn at different times. And there are over 120 species of trees in the park. Dogwoods, for example, tend to turn early. Second, the exposure of a tree—for example, southern or northern—affects the angle and the amount of sunlight it receives. Third, the elevation at which a tree grows affects the weather in which it grows, which in turn affects when the tree changes color. Together these factors produce an evolving mixture of hues.

Just a few strokes of fall's artistry tinged the predominantly pine pathway as it approached Abrams Creek. In the next mile, after crossing a few rhododendron-choked feeder streams, I neared the Little Bottoms campsite. Every campsite in the Smokies has a name and a corresponding number on the trail map. Little Bottoms is number seventeen. It is a popular fishing camp, located atop a small hill at an old homesite, safe from flood-prone Abrams Creek. Rock walls, rock piles, and even an old chimney look somewhat out of place as forest succession occurs. First, some type of bush—blueberry, for instance—invades an open site. Sun-loving trees like black locust follow the bushes. Finally, hardwoods come in and claim their place.

Due to the likelihood of rain, I raised a shelter under a small stand of pines. After stringing a small rope between two trees, I placed my eight-by-ten-foot sheet of clear plastic over it. Then I put heavy rocks on two corners of the plastic, where I planned to lay my head, and tied the other two corners two feet above the base of nearby trees. The result was an airy, rainproof enclave.

I endorse the use of tarps. They are easily erected in a number of shapes, adaptable to any situation. They can be set up as a windbreak to cook by or low to the ground in a heavy rain. They are easy to get into and out of, having no doors or zippers, are light and simple to carry, and provide a cheery atmosphere, letting in natural light. And a tarp costs only a tenth as much as even the cheapest tent. Under the versatile shelter went my pack; then I assembled my Diawa backpack fishing rod. It breaks into several pieces, fitting into a breadloaf-sized box. I pocketed my plastic film canister of lures, changed into my canvas hightop "fishing" shoes, and hit the creek. I must add that felt-soled shoes are much safer, though more costly.

To many fly-fishing anglers, spinner-fishing for trout is a crude insult to a noble pursuit, but I do not agree. Most creeks in the Smokies are heavily canopied overhead, with additional dense growth along their banks. Little room is left in which to toss a lot of line around with a long rod. A spinning rod is shorter, and very little slack line is needed to place the lure in the desired location. To fly-fishermen, casting a fly with a long pole is poetry in motion. To me, spinner-fishing is the same, but I cast a larger lure with a shorter pole. Looking good is not the goal. The goal is catching fish.

I tied a white Roostertail on my line and began fishing up the creek. Just as the rush of getting on the creek began to dissipate and my mind turned to the sights and smells of fall, a rainbow caught me. I was reeling in my lure through a fast, deep current, and my line tightened. Jerked back from my sightseeing, I set the hook and reeled in a colorful rainbow that brightened the gray day. In short order I caught and released two more fish before a steady rain began and I returned to camp.

The rain cooled things off. It was just below sixty degrees as I changed into dry trousers and T-shirt under a long-sleeved work shirt. It was imperative that I keep myself and especially my gear as dry as possible, since I had five nights out ahead of me. No matter how careful a backpacker is during a rain lasting several days, clothes and gear slowly get wetter and wetter, becoming difficult to dry and demanding more effort to tote. At 2:30 P.M., I settled under my secure shelter and began to read the Knoxville newspaper. But the rhythm of the rain on the tarp soon lulled me into a cozy nap.

A loud crash startled me awake at dusk. A tree had fallen nearby. If a tree falls in the woods, it makes a loud sound; I heard it. Though the rain had subsided, I ruled out building a fire, deciding to boil my hot dogs for supper rather than roasting them over the fire. But first I needed an eye-opening cup of java. In the lantern's glow, while sipping the coffee, I absently boiled the wieners; then, happily, I remembered having brought mustard, which would lend flavor to an otherwise bland meal. Simple pleasures take on added significance out in the woods.

After supper I resumed reading the paper, while enjoying a little country music on my portable transistor radio. Backpackers are rarely neutral on the subject of a radio in the wilds. I enjoy listening to news, sports, and especially old-time greats like George Jones while relaxing at the campsite. Weather information can be vital, especially on a long trip that extends beyond the forecast on the day you set out. My nature experience is not diluted, because I can always turn off the radio. Around nine that night, I put out the lantern and slipped into my bag, vowing to get an early start in the morning. The light rain that resumed helped me sleep soundly through the night.

I arose at first light, glad of a halt in the precipitation, though the morning loomed dark, wet, and cloudy. To complement my coffee, I scrambled some eggs and toasted a bagel for breakfast. Bagels are a good bread choice, being small, compact, and firm, so they don't take up much room and won't get mashed in your pack. I shook the water off my tarp, compactly folded it, packed the rest of my gear, and continued southeast on the Little Bottoms Trail, which traversed a rocky, piney stretch of the steep-sided valley.

The difficulty of the trail made me think of a shortcut. Not far beyond the campsite, amid a rocky outcrop far above Abrams

Creek, I spotted the shortcut between two small bushes, as it had been described by a local man I had run into on a previous camping trip to Little Bottoms. The trail led up to the Hatcher Mountain Trail, saving "at least a mile of roundabout hiking," according to my source. Well, the "trail" petered out after about a hundred yards, but I kept pressing up the steep hill, zigzagging under the weight of my pack. On a really tough climb, I will sometimes stop and lean over, hands on my knees, catch my breath, and then continue. After such a rest, with fifteen minutes of heavy panting, I came to the real trail and continued up Hatcher Mountain, but on a much gentler grade. I rounded the mountain and then descended to cross tiny Oak Flats Branch, nestled in a copse of sodden dark hemlock trees.

Beyond the rill, the trailside woods were still green, despite the many deciduous trees interspersed among the evergreens. Deciduous trees are what make autumn spectacular in the Smokies. The green chlorophyll in the leaves fades, revealing the leaf pigment underneath. Then the leaves drop, leaving branches bare for the dormant winter season. Hickory, oak, and dogwood are well-known examples of deciduous trees. White pine is the predominant evergreen on the Hatcher Mountain Trail, which I followed from Little Bottoms for three and a half miles, to intersect the Cooper Road Trail again, on its way to Cades Cove. I pushed forward and picked up the Beard Cane Trail, at an elevation of nineteen hundred feet. The trail leads northeast through an area known as the "Hurricane," named after a terrible storm that blew through long ago. Beard Cane Mountain and Hatcher Mountain parallel the trail on its journey to Hesse Creek.

After a short walk to and then through Beard Cane Gap, I wound my way down to Beard Cane Creek, so named for the native bamboo—at one time harvested for fishing poles—that grows in the valley. The trail and the creek crisscross many times, often intermingling, so that mud-slopping, rock-hopping, and log-crossing are to be expected on this lightly traveled trail.

A little over an hour into the agility test known as the Beard Cane Trail, I floundered my way to a relatively wide area marking an old logging camp, now reforested. Beyond this former camp, I could hear the rush of the louder and larger Hesse Creek, into which Beard Cane Creek runs. Forty-six creek crossings were behind me; the Hesse Creek campsite was not far. The campsite, situated inside a bend of the creek, may be the flattest campsite in the park. I arrived near noon and quickly unpacked my gear beneath a towering white pine. As I boiled water with my Svea stove, I watched the sky above. Black, low-slung clouds spelled only rain. So much for the dry October theory.

I grabbed my rod and lures, then covered my pack with the tarp. Suddenly I noticed that there was only one tennis shoe strapped to my pack. The other must have fallen off somewhere along the trail. I was out a shoe and was a litterbug, too. I could only hope that a thoughtful hiker would pack it out. When strapping items on the outside of your backpack, check your work. Not only can they fall off of their own accord, but grabby trees and brush can pick them off as well. Now I would have to fish in my hiking boots, rendering them wet for days. Yet, had I stayed in camp pouting over not being able to fish Hesse Creek, a misery far worse than wet boots would have overcome me.

Now I set my fishing plan in motion. I crossed Hesse Creek, then climbed uphill half a mile to Blair Gap, at the park's boundary. On previous occasions I had noticed an old unmaintained trail heading westward. It coincided with a trail, seen on some maps, that doubles back to Hesse Creek downstream from the campsite. I would follow the unmaintained trail to Hesse Creek, then fish my way upstream to the campsite.

The plan was rife with uncertainty. What if the unmaintained trail did not lead to Hesse Creek? How long would it take to get there, even if it did lead to Hesse Creek? How long would it take to fish my way up to the campsite? What would I do if darkness fell and I was stuck on the trailless creek? I had tried to answer these questions before I left home, by studying a topographical map of the area. I estimated that the whole event, if all went well, would take six hours. Yet one question lingered: when would the rain resume?

This last question was answered immediately. A sprinkle commenced as I set out from Blair Gap on the constricted brush-lined trail. As I went along, I was startled to see fresh horse manure on the path. Later, while rounding a hill forested with impressive hardwoods, I encountered a large fallen hickory blocking the way. Yet, upon closer inspection, I saw that a chainsaw had cleared a small passage through the huge downed tree. Apparently a local horseman sporadically tended this "unmaintained" trail.

I felt increasingly convinced that this was the old Hurricane Mountain Trail, which positively led down to Hesse Creek. Sure enough, in a little over an hour, I left the ridge top and found myself at Hesse Creek where, at its most northwesterly flow, it exits from the park. I quietly began fishing my way up the small creek, carefully casting my lure at the head of the first pool I encountered. I reeled the Roostertail in across the pool at a pace slightly faster than the creek's current and hooked a fighting ten-inch rainbow trout. A wily trout, if given any slack, will spit out a hook, or jump and get off. But this one could not escape. I placed the fish on my stringer and excitedly waded upstream.

The misty drizzle did not dampen my enthusiasm. The rain striking the vivid leaves sang a song that could be heard only in the woods and only while the leaves were still on the trees. On its journey to the forest floor, a raindrop may hop down, from leaf to leaf, all the way to the ground, creating a cascading sound. During leafless winter, raindrops more often travel straight to the ground, making a pounding sound that becomes more subdued as the leaves on the ground disintegrate.

Once again I turned my attention to fishing. I landed some battling smallmouths, along with many small trout, that I put back to be caught another day. I could not help noticing the loveliness of this intimate creek valley. Dripping rhododendron lined the gin-clear stream, interspersed with mossy gray rocks. Fall colors tinged the misty canopy of trees.

The fishing foray had its drawbacks, however. Between wading the creek and being chilled by rain and air, I grew cold. I realized that the initial stage of hypothermia was on the horizon. Eventually my hands became so numb that I could hardly operate the reel. As the sky grew portentously darker, I stumbled upstream against the flow of water, fishing each hole briefly. The distance to camp was unknown. Yet I maintained composure, knowing that rushing blindly upstream in the growing darkness might well result in injury. Panic, miscalculation, and injury follow one upon another in the wilderness. Often, when facing adversity, a hiker may rashly rush off, trying to find the way or to get help, becoming disoriented or injured and making the original problem even worse.

Luck was on my side that day. Just as it became dangerously dark, I made my way into the campsite in the gloomy fog. Even the rain had diminished to an almost imperceptible mist. But I had made my luck. The map study had paid off, and my travel calculations had been correct. My hands and feet were nearly numb, but I had kept my wits about me even as the chilly night enveloped me. And in one of those nearly numb hands I held a stringer of five healthy rainbow trout.

I cast the rod and stringer aside, dug my headlamp out of my pack, and began the arduous task of making a fire. I moved quickly and constantly while gathering the wet wood, in an effort to warm up as well as get the task done. There is an old saying: wood warms you three times—while you gather it, while you break it apart, and while you burn it. Using part of the newspaper I had already read and some semidry twigs found near the base of a small hemlock tree, I ignited the fire. I nursed the flame and then turned my attention to cleaning fish. By lamplight at the water's edge, I beheaded, gutted, and rinsed them. Finally I changed into dry clothes. I had my goosedown booties to wear instead of wet boots. The dry duds felt great after six hours in clinging, wet clothes in a fifty-degree drizzle. I could have safely huddled beneath the tarp all day, keeping my boots and my body dry, but the calculated risk had been worth it. Often a part of a Smoky Mountain experience, rain is not something to shy away from.

Now it was time to cook. I set my greased frying pan (actually a nonsticking pie tin) over the whirring stove and in the pan placed the fresh trout, laden with garlic and pepper, two at a time. After sautéing the fish until the skin became crisp, I set them on some remaining newspaper to drain. I feasted on fresh

Smoky Mountain trout, triumphantly tossing the bones into the fire. The meal had been well worth the effort. I made a post-dinner cup of coffee and at 10 P.M. finally relaxed before the crackling fire. What a day! I had barely stopped moving since dawn. This was no respite from work.

I had only one regret. I regretted not setting the tarp before the fishing excursion. This final chore was accomplished haphazardly at best. After placing all my gear under the tarp, I stretched out in my bag and read the paper with my headlamp for about twelve seconds, until I dropped into a deep sleep. The rain fell heavily during the night, but my shelter held, and I stayed dry.

At daylight, the forest was drenched, and my thermometer read just forty-five degrees. I had slept soundly and was ready for my twelve-mile day. I greeted the dismal morning with a cup of hot coffee, topped off with some powdered milk. Don't add powdered milk directly to coffee; mix it with cold water first, then add it. Four scrambled eggs and a toasted bagel comprised the rest of my breakfast. At 9 A.M. I doused the fire and broke camp. I tied my boots together by their laces, draped them over my shoulders with the laces behind my neck, and waded barefoot across Hesse Creek, which had risen several inches during the night. I put on dry socks and my still-damp boots, then once again climbed up to Blair Gap. But this time I veered east on the Ace Gap Trail, roughly paralleling a section of the park's northern boundary.

Although this was my third day out, the abundance of remaining food and my wet clothing and gear weighed heavily upon my back. The ridge-running Ace Gap Trail, which ranges in elevation from fifteen hundred to two thousand feet, displayed more colorful leaves along its six-mile stretch to Rich Mountain Gap than had the trees in the creek valleys. Passing through Ace Gap, I found it hard to accept that a railroad once had run through this hushed, tree-choked woodland down to the logging camp back on Hesse Creek. In the Smokies, moisture, soil, temperature, and altitude variation combine to make ideal growing conditions for a variety of trees which compete

ALONG THE ACE GAP TRAIL. The ridge-running Ace Gap Trail, which ranges in elevation from 1,500 to 2,000 feet, displayed more colorful leaves along its six-mile run to Rich Mountain Gap than the trees in the creek valleys.

for light in the forest. The result is incredibly dense growth. That is why it does not take long for the Smokies to conceal old railroad beds, homesites, and abandoned trails.

Leaving the gap under a sky the color of gunmetal, I reached the high point on the trail just as a white-tailed deer darted into a laurel thicket. I wove my way downward and entered a fog bank that obscured the brushy pathway. Since this was a lightly traveled trail, the laurel had grown up, and I unsuccessfully dodged between the overhanging branches, which soaked me as I passed. With fog shrouding Kelly Gap, location of a backcountry campsite and a fine spring, I dropped my pack there. Having traveled five miles from Hesse Creek, I drank the cool mountain spring water and rested.

Renewed, I shouldered my backpack again and left Kelly Gap. The trail led through a burned-out area. Table Mountain pine trunks displayed their contrasting black bases. Firefighters apparently used the trail as a firebreak, because the north side obviously had been burned, while the south side had no visible fire scars on the tree trunks and the understory was thick with trailing arbutus and galax.

Fire plays an important role in pine and pine-oak forests like the one in which I was traveling. Eventually the piney woods will mature, leaving little room for new trees and much duff on the ground. Then a fire, sparked by lightning, will burn over the area, and the dead trees will rot and give new plants the nutrients and light necessary for growth. The cycle will begin again. This is why old-growth forests of pine are rare—the trees usually burn before they become really large.

Past the burned area, I came to Rich Mountain Gap, immediately crossed Rich Mountain Road, and began climbing up the south slope of Rich Mountain. This peak is named for the dense, luxuriant growth that clothes its heights. As the trail meandered two miles upward, it crisscrossed both the southern and northern slopes of the ridge, revealing a continuum of fall color. I entered the tunnel of a rhododendron thicket at the headwaters of Hesse Creek, which at this point is a trickling spring that could not support a school of minnows.

Shortly thereafter, the trail intersected the Indian Grave

Gap Trail and followed it for half a mile to Rich Mountain's pinnacle, where a fire tower once stood at an elevation of 3,680 feet. You can still see its four concrete support bases. To the northwest lies the nearby park border town of Townsend, Tennessee. And to the south stands the bulk of the Smokies. I was enchanted with the state of the leaves at this higher elevation; the peak was ablaze with red, orange, and yellow leaves turning the once-green mountaintop into a fall cornucopia of color.

I decided to take a break on the vivid crest. The day had warmed quite nicely, to a balmy sixty-five degrees, though the clouds hung heavy and foreboding overhead, like a white blanket. I snacked on saltines covered with peanut butter and a couple of Moon Pies. Given the sinister state of the sky, I was fortunate to avoid rain. I grudgingly moved down the trail, as my muscles had stiffened slightly during the break, but was rewarded with many views into lush and somber Cades Cove. Beyond the cove, the towering crest of the Smokies stood guard over its domain. Just one and a half miles from the mountaintop, I reached the Scott Mountain Trail, down which I hiked my last hundred yards of the day to the Turkey Pen Ridge campsite.

I had anticipated feeling joy and relief upon seeing the small campsite, just a runty flat spot thirty-four hundred feet high on the ridge. Instead, a wave of loneliness engulfed me. I had camped here before, but this time the place looked desolate. It was not the site itself, of course, but my state of mind. The swarthy afternoon only intensified my mood. I unshouldered my pack, telling myself to shake it off and get on with my camp chores. As I walked down to the nearby spring, I had to fight off an urge to rush down through barren hardwoods to Cades Cove and somehow get back to the Jeep. Instead, I filled my water bag and resolved to make a fire. That would help keep me busy and cheer me up. That is just what I did, and it did. Then I pulled out my stove and made a soothing cup of hot chocolate. Before long I was hypnotized by the flames dancing in the late afternoon dusk; the woodland once more was my ally.

I have spent many nights alone, and the vast bulk of my experiences have been positive ones. I have learned self-reliance and been given plenty of time to think. Everyone owes it to herself or himself to spend a few days alone in the woods. Doing so, you learn much about who you are.

After supper, under the lantern, I reclined against a fallen oak, the fire warming my front side, and read a *National Geographic* I had stored in the recesses of my pack. The woods are an ideal distraction-free place to read, and any book or magazine I bring along is well worth its weight. If the need arises, I always can use already-read pages to start a fire, reducing weight at the same time.

Around 10 P.M., I readied my sleeping area. I laid out my sleeping pad on a spot cleared of pebbles, then spread out my sleeping bag. That is as far as I go in site maintenance—the days of trenching around the tent are over. Just in case of rain, I covered my pack with my ground sheet and placed my tarp beside me. I turned out my lantern and quickly fell asleep. It was a good thing I had my tarp with me, because the rain came. In a semiconscious state, I threw the plastic over me and slumbered once again. This method works in a pinch, but it is a most unpleasant feeling to wake up choking, with cold plastic blocking your breathing passages.

That is how my fourth morning dawned. At least it was not still raining. As I sipped a cup of hot chocolate in the forty-five-degree chill, menacing clouds still hovered over the Smokies. After breakfasting quickly, I packed my gear and scanned the campsite for litter. I laced my arms into my backpack and retraced the hundred yards back to the Rich Mountain Trail. There I began the two-and-a-half-mile descent into Cades Cove along several switchbacks. Fog covered the floor of the cove, as I could see from several vantage points on the way down.

By 10 A.M. I reached the cove, which was full of cars and people—mostly people in cars, all here for the fall foliage display. People in cars gawked at me, and I returned the favor. We were having completely different Smoky Mountain experiences. I had seen only nature, not one human being, since I began; I had been touching, feeling, smelling—absorbing—the very essence of these highlands. I wished that the "windshield visitors" could have been doing the same. Auto touring has its advantages, of course. You can see a lot of territory in a short period of time, but you see it only fleetingly and at a distance. A grand view is rewarding, but so is, for example, watching a spider lying in wait for its prey on the edge of a dewy web stretched across a backwoods trail. That cannot be seen by car. Auto tourists would have an even better experience if they left their cars behind and went *into* the mountains.

I followed my own advice and swept through the Cades Cove picnic area as rapidly as possible, to reach the Anthony Creek trailhead. I marched right back into the woods. This popular trail, which on this day I had to myself, leads to Spence Field on the AT, at the crest of the Smokies. I followed it for a mile and a half to the Russell Field Trail junction, where I ran into three teenagers who looked much the worse for wear. This had been their first backpacking trip, they told me. They had bitten off more than they could chew, as first-timers often do. Good planning is critical for a successful overnight hike. But at least they were attempting something. Every old-timer was once a novice.

Once on the Russell Field Trail, I trudged upward through a mature hardwood forest with many large hemlocks all around. During the ensuing mile to the Leadbetter Ridge campsite, three thousand feet above sea level, I encountered several mud puddles in the trail. Now, it is best for the trail to stay on it wherever possible. Occasionally I go around mud puddles, but doing so just widens the trail, which increases the muddy area.

The Leadbetter Ridge campsite, at the trail's last reliable water source, was a good place for a break. I shed my backpack, retrieving some snacks from a side pocket. The rest revitalized me for the final push up to Russell Field.

I left the valley and ascended onto Leadbetter Ridge, traversing a level stretch lined with mountain laurel almost continuously for a mile. The trail became very steep for a short, exhausting stretch leading into Russell Field, a melancholy ooze under the pulsing, ashen sky. Shortly past noon, I propped my pack up with a broken tree limb out in the open and sauntered to the spring that Russell Sparks had used when he stayed up here, 4,360 feet on top of old Smoky. Sometimes after an all-day hike, walking around packless feels like walking without gravity. As I returned to my pack, full water bottle in hand, the clouds began to break apart. Minutes later, I was basking in the sun, watching the sky turn blue. The sunshine made Russell Field positively radiant. The brown grass of the former pasture glinted in the rays of the autumn sun. I stripped to my shorts and laid all my wet clothes out to dry atop my ground sheet. The steam rising from my damp clothing drifted away like a bad dream.

At 3:30, I began trekking westward on the AT, straddling the Tennessee–North Carolina border, after passing the crowded Russell Field shelter. I hoped that my intended destination, Mollies Ridge shelter, would not be similarly occupied. A rigorous climb, followed by a spiraling descent, led me into Big Abrams Gap and back out in a lung-bursting climb. A strong wind kicked up, drying and cooling my sweaty body. This up-and-down terrain was wearing me thin as I passed yet another example of fall's beauty—a brilliant stand of beech trees, draped in golden leaves fluttering at the wind's whim. Curiously, younger beech trees keep their leaves through the winter, though they are dried and brown. This feature makes the tree easy for people to identify. But animals of the Smokies, such as deer, turkey, and bear, know this tree well, for it provides them with the beechnut, an important food in their diet.

I halted at the Devil's Tater Patch, 4,750 feet up, and rested my throbbing muscles. A fog abruptly swept over the ridge top, reducing my visibility to a scant twenty yards in all directions. I wandered on through the rolling fog. Finally the Mollies Ridge shelter came into view, and for a moment I wondered if I had entered the Twilight Zone. I stared at the surrounding scene in disbelief and then in alarm. Ten to fifteen horses of all sizes and colors were tied up around the shelter. A band of horsemen, all heavily bearded, wearing long range coats, and looking as if they had stepped right out of the 1880s, lurked in front of the shelter. The unfriendly stares of the group left me feeling self-conscious. The welcome mat had just been jerked up. I said "howdy" and just kept moving. Later I found out that the group had been roving unrestrained through the Smokies, raising a ruckus. Park rangers were hunting them.

The unexpected encounter with shelter bandits had altered my plans. I did not want to camp in an undesignated area, but the "long riders" were not about to share that shelter. Sundown was near, and I did not know where to camp. A long, steep descent ended at Ekaneetlee Gap, one of the lowest spots on the Smokies' crest (elevation 3,842 feet), a mile past the marauders of Mollies Ridge. Although it was illegal to do so, I decided to camp there. To hike on to a designated site would necessitate too much night hiking. Staying there was the safest decision. And the place had both of the qualifications I require in a campsite: a flat spot and water.

There was a dripping spring a hundred yards down the Tennessee side of the gap. While I got water from it, darkness fell on the spare crest. I lit my lantern, which imparted a soupy complexion to the foggy evening. A fire was out of the question. I felt bad enough camping illegally right on the AT; to build a fire ring and burn the vegetation down to the soil would have been unconscionable. I sipped hot chocolate and coffee in the cool night air. I prepared a late dinner of tuna and noodles, which in my sleepy state I had trouble finishing.

It was a cool forty degrees when I awoke. I warmed up with several cups of coffee, ate a few buttered bagel halves toasted in the frying pan for breakfast, broke camp, and departed an hour after sunrise. The thick fog hung in the mountain air while I climbed out of Ekaneetlee Gap to Doe Knob, gaining seven hundred feet in one and four-tenths miles. I traveled rapidly, as my pack, with less food and no wet clothes, now was much lighter. It seemed that I was losing weight, too, as sweat poured off me despite the cool temperature. Due to the fog, visibility was limited, but that hardly mattered, for my eyes stared at the ground and my head hung down as I gasped for air on the sharp upgrade.

The sun greeted me at Doe Knob, where the AT veers south to scale Shuckstack Mountain and cross Fontana Lake at Fontana Dam. In the days before the dam was constructed, the AT continued westward, continuing to shadow the Tennessee–North Carolina border and eventually leaving the park at Deals Gap. The trail was rerouted when Fontana Lake was created in the early 1940s. The old AT is now called the Gregory Bald Trail, which I followed two miles to its next trail intersection at Rich Gap. This gap is known to old-timer natives as Gant Lot. They say that there used to be, in the gap, a large fenced area where cattle, after spending the summer grazing on grassy nearby mountaintops, became "gaunted" while waiting to make it out of the mountains to market.

At the gap I took a side trail leading seventy-five yards to Moore Spring, site of an old AT shelter. The spring is reputed to be one of the best in the Smokies, and I testify on its behalf. I sat in the sunny glade, eating lunch and feeling really good about where I was and what I was doing. A woodpecker pounded intently in the distance. Many AT hikers in the pre-1940 era had stopped at this place. They had had a lot tougher time traveling than we do now. Portable camp stoves were unheard of, and what gear they had was heavy and bulky. A quick look at today's gear reveals that the majority of it consists of lightweight plastic. When I think I have it tough, I remember the trailblazers of yesteryear; that keeps everything in perspective.

I slipped my arms under the shoulder straps of my pack, reluctantly left the spring, and climbed the last three-quarters of a mile up to Gregory Bald. This open, grassy "bald," 4,950 feet up, is known worldwide for its display of flame azaleas in June. It also offers awesome mountain views in nearly all directions.

In recent years, Gregory Bald has undergone some changes. At the time of the park's creation, it consisted of fifteen acres of grassy field. By the 1980s, it was less than half that size, having grown over, like many of the park's balds. Then the Park Service decided to restore and maintain Gregory Bald and Andrews Bald. Park employees set about cutting the small trees and the blueberry and hawthorn bushes back and burning the cuttings. Native grass was replanted, and now the bald is maintained at its original size. The Park Service would like to leave nature alone whenever possible, but in this case it decided, for scenic, historic, and environmental reasons, to interfere. In such cases, people have to decide how much human intervention should be allowed to alter nature's course.

Fall from Gregory Bald. Color-splashed ridges stretched off in all directions.

Cades Cove, clearly visible three thousand feet below, looked close enough to touch. Here and there, autumn trees looked almost electrically brilliant. Color-splashed ridges stretched off in all directions. The abundant remaining blueberry bushes had become blood-purple balls of fire. The warm sun and cool air mixed, giving my skin the most exhilarating feeling. I stopped and shot some photos that I would later label "Fall in the Smokies." Then I relaxed in the sun for about an hour. I left the bald around 1 P.M., with miles to go before I slept.

Upon leaving the sunny field, I re-entered the hardwood forest and soon came to Sheep Pen Gap, location of a backcountry campsite. The Gregory Bald Trail veered northwest and descended past a series of tiny springs choked with freshly fallen leaves. The dry leafy aroma filled my nostrils. On the three-and-a-half-mile downswing from the state boundary, I moved easily and steadily down to Sams Gap. As I hiked, I watched sunlight and shade play tag among the colorful windblown leaves, as the closed oak forest gave way to pine.

The way things are going, it will not stay pine forever. Since this old-growth forest area came under national park supervision and protection, natural fires have been suppressed. As a result, the forest is undergoing succession from primarily pine and pine-oak to oak and other hardwoods. After the big fire in Yellowstone in the late 1980s, prescribed-area burning has gained in popularity, but it has not been undertaken in the Smokies. By "protecting" this section of virgin park land from fire, the Park Service is forcing a change in forest type. By igniting prescribed burns, however, it would alter nature. So, either way, these woods are not allowed to continue naturally. One solution would be to let natural fires burn as they occur, but this could be a big gamble if the fires raged out of control, especially with the historic wooden structures of Cades Cove nearby. The dilemma has no clear-cut solution.

Even though the ascent out of Sams Gap was gentle, the intermittent sunlight and the afternoon warmth left me sweating profusely. I cooled down somewhat as the piney trail peaked out about a mile from the gap and I hiked on down the virgin wooded slopes of Hannah Mountain. Two miles beyond the high point of the mountain, the trail descended steeply through sun-dappled woodland, passing several small, cool creeks, to arrive one mile further at the Flint Gap campsite. The campsite, at 2,050 feet, is one of the least used and most isolated campsites in the park. It is quite small—indeed, just a wide spot on the Hannah Mountain Trail.

After dropping my pack, I backtracked up the trail to the last watercourse I had crossed and filled my waterbag. Back at camp, I relaxed in a sliver of sunlight and brewed a cup of java while listening to the sounds of the fall woods—birds, blowing leaves, wind. My sunny rest did not last long, however, as the sun fell behind the surrounding mountainside and took the temperature with it. I easily collected wood and started a fire.

As the day drew to a close, I sat still in front of the flames. Suddenly my head spun to the side, as I heard leaves rustling loudly about thirty yards away. Down into the gap ambled a small black bear, probably a yearling, unaware of my presence. It crunched over the dead remnants of summer foliage. At ten yards it finally spotted me; our eyes met, and for a moment all was quiet and still, save for the crackling fire. Then the bear shot up the ridge side, making more noise than ever. That reaction bodes well for the bear. The farther it stays from man, the better its chances of a long life.

I prepared a glamorous dinner of macaroni and cheese. The powdered milk made it thick enough to taste good. Actually, on the fifth night of a strenuous backpacking trip, fried sawdust patties sound edible. I wolfed down the hot, filling slop as the night came on. Lying on my back, I watched the stars emerge from the twilight. Veiled by day, the ancient points of light emerged one by one until the night sky was aglow with other worlds. I returned to earth and decided to light my lantern to read, although my fuel supply was nearly depleted. But the lantern lasted another two hours, enough time to finish my *National Geographic*. On this trip, my gas needs had been estimated well. While backpacking, you don't want to carry unnecessary weight, but you don't want to run out of whatever you need, either.

Lying in the dark, snug in my bag, I knew that the next and final day would be fairly easy. It had been a fun, eventful trip, and, as was usual toward the end of a hike, while lying in my bag awaiting sleep, I found my thoughts turning back to town.

A cool, sunny morning came to Flint Gap. I unzipped my sleeping bag and began my last day. It was forty-five degrees as I lit my stove and brewed a cup of coffee. I spread cream cheese on my last bagel, then ate it while packing up. Something like cream cheese can keep for days in such weather. Store it in the recesses of your pack during the heat of the day and out where it can cool down at night, and it will be fine.

Clad only in shorts and a T-shirt, I left the gap behind, hurrying along to warm up in the brisk morning. I maintained the swift pace during the three-mile, mostly downward trek to Scott Gap and my last trail junction. The sunny day had warmed somewhat as I turned northwestward on an old woods road for the short climb up Pine Mountain, (elevation 2,100 feet). From the top of Pine Mountain, travel was easy. It was all downhill on an open Jeep trail to the Abrams Creek ranger station. But a long downgrade can be irritating in its own way. Your knees and feet take a pounding, and you must be careful not to twist an ankle. The backpack, bouncing up and down on your shoulders, can be really annoying. But your lungs do not mind the descent one bit.

Soon I crossed the narrow footbridge over Abrams Creek and hiked the last hundred yards back to the Jeep. Having just completed a fifty-mile loop around the perimeter of Cades Cove, I felt mixed emotions; I was glad the trip was completed but sorry to leave autumn in the Great Smokies. I knew that I would be back for more.

Thanksgiving in the Mountains

Thomas Divide to Deep Creek

As I cracked open the door of my Jeep, a gust of wind jerked the door handle out of my hand. Frigid air blasted into the vehicle. This was going to be a chilly trip. It was Thanksgiving Day, and I was on Newfound Gap Road, three and a half miles into North Carolina, at the top end of the Thomas Divide Trail in the Great Smoky Mountains National Park. As I approached the trailhead, I wondered who else would be backpacking on a subfreezing holiday. I knew of one such person, my longtime friend and hiking partner, Steve Grayson, who was to meet me at the first night's campsite, Newton Bald.

I started on the trail at 1 P.M. The afternoon was sunsplashed, but with a weak, white sun. In shady spots, a light coating of snow covered both the trail and the fallen leaves on the forest floor. No telltale footprints of other hikers appeared on the white ground. The rhododendron leaves were curled tight as a testament to the chill. The ridge-running trail gently rose and fell, reaching its highest point at Turkey Flyup (elevation 5,160 feet), a little over a mile from the trailhead. The barren forest allowed views of surrounding ragged ridges and valleys, no longer softened by the green leaves of summer.

I was plenty warmed up from hiking and so decided to stop for a minute and take off my gloves. Leaning against an old maple tree, I listened to the woods. Above, the air, borne by the north wind, whipped through the high tree branches. On the ground the snow-covered leaves lay still. No creature stirred within earshot. My pack thermometer read twenty-four degrees, the highest it would register all day. I moved on; there was still a good bit of ridge between the campsite and me.

In a short distance I bolted through the Kanati Fork Trail junction. In my haste I nearly fell, as a ruffled grouse exploded in flight before me. Each time this occurs, it startles the unsuspecting hiker. Often you cannot see a grouse, but you can identify their presence by the strange thudding sound they make, known as drumming. This curious sound, which initially I thought was the creaking of tree trunks in the wind, is made by the birds beating their wings. You have never seen a better routine on stage than a mother grouse doing her wounded bird act to protect her nearby brood from intruders. Though found in lower coves and valleys, the grouse reaches its greatest numbers in the rough and high mountain regions.

The day was short, and I wanted to get to the campsite with time to make a fire before dark. Still, I slowed down so as to make it in one piece. Past the junction I climbed to the top of Nettle Creek Bald, one of many balds whose wooded tops now belie their names. Three miles into the hike, I descended to Tuskee Gap. I marched southward along the ridge, as my pack, laden with provisions, began to weigh heavy on my shoulders. The initial thrill that accompanies the beginning of a backpacking trip was wearing off. My nose was cold, too.

I reached the junction with the Sunkota Ridge Trail and continued south, still on Thomas Divide, another half-mile to the Newton Bald Trail. For the most part, trail intersections in the Smokies are well marked with wooden signs telling trail names and pertinent distances. Veering west, I bounced happily along, knowing that the Newton Bald campsite was a mere tenth of a mile away. The Newton Bald campsite actually is in a narrow, windswept gap five thousand feet high, due west of the overgrown Newton Bald. I dropped my pack by the lone fire ring at 3 P.M. The sun's scant heat was already waning as I took my water bottle and waterbag down the steep south side of the gap to a small spring. Erroneously, the Park Service and the Sierra Club's guide to the Smokies state that this campsite has no water.

While filling my waterbag in the chilly shade, I heard rustling off to one side. I froze, eager to see what it was. Then, only twenty feet away, five wild boars rooted through the frosty leaves, snorting loudly. I moved closer, but they noticed me and moved off; I could still hear them, though. The big, hairy, tusked boars were an intimidating sight, but they generally shun encounters with humans. A boar encounter is rare indeed.

I toted the water back up to the gap. I was pleasantly surprised to see Steve at the campsite. He knew that I was already at camp, having seen my Jeep and then my footprints on the trail. We instantly set about gathering wood. Plenty was available, as this campsite was lightly used, especially in the cold season. Before I started the fire, I rearranged the fire ring into a rectangular shape instead of the traditional but impractical circle. Here are the facts as I have found them. Smoke seldom rises straight up above the fire. If campers sit in a circular arrangement around the fire, someone is going to get smoked out, so campers end up sitting on one side of the fire, anyway. In arranging the fire ring in a rectangular shape, you facilitate the laying of wood for the fire. The wood, when broken up, is laid best in a crisscross pattern, to allow the fire optimum oxygen. Campers sit alongside the fire, out of the smoke, instead of around it in the smoke.

I stacked three of the largest logs at the back of the fire ring, across from where we would sit. Those back logs would burn slowly, reflecting the fire's heat back at us, as well as forcing the smoke higher in the air and away from us. A fire bellowing smoke in your face is worse than no fire at all. I then ignited the fire, while Steve broke the rest of the wood into pieces small enough to fit in the fire ring. While Steve tended and built up the blaze, I unfolded and erected my tent. Little chance existed of precipitation, but Newton Bald campsite was known to be windy; hence the tent. Through the window of my tent, I could see the crest of the Smokies, particularly the road cut on the side of Clingman's Dome. The sun was sinking fast, the wind blowing steadily. This day of thanks was coming to a close.

In pre-park days, Christmas was the big holiday. Mountaineers had less then; a lone toy and some fruit might be all that Santa left for children in the Smokies. A big meal was as much of a tradition then as it is now.

I returned to the comforting fire and lit my Coleman lantern. By 5:45 the sun was totally gone, even from the ridgetops, where the sun shines latest. I made a pot of coffee and then stirred in hot chocolate mix, a flavorful brew and, in the cup, an effective hand warmer.

Steve demanded that his stomach be filled with a big meal. I retrieved my stove from the backpack. Before I lit the stove, I used some spare wood and made a windbreak, then placed the stove on the protected side of the wooden windbreak. A stove will use considerably less fuel out of the wind, where the heat can rise directly under the pot rather than being blown away from it. I heated a leftover meal of kielbasa, red beans, and rice. One big advantage of cold weather hiking is that you can bring perishable food and be confident that it will stay well "refrigerated."

As Steve and I ate, we heard a stir in the distance. Just as we began to worry about what the noise might be, a group of four Alabamans, two couples, appeared out of the darkness. They were glad to see that we had a fire, for the temperature, driven downward by a raw wind, now was below twenty degrees. As the women toasted by the fire, the men borrowed my lantern and struck up their tents. It turned out that each year they come up for a Thanksgiving hike; this year, however, they had been delayed on the way up and thus were stuck hiking at night. The six of us sat by the blazing fire, comparing notes on our experiences in the Smokies.

Around 10 P.M., the couples retired. I moved the lantern into our tent, suspending it by rope and covering it with a piece of foil to slow and spread the heat it dispensed. I unzipped the windows some, to make sure the lantern would not use up all the oxygen in the tent. This process will warm a tent ten degrees or more. There is a psychological lift when the temperature is warmer inside than outside. But you cannot be too careful using a lantern inside a tent. I placed the waterbag between

FRIGID MORNING AT NEWTON BALD CAMPSITE. With the hot coffee, the fire, and the sunshine, I was as warm as anyone could be on such a frozen Smoky Mountain morning.

the fire and our sitting log, hoping that it would not freeze completely overnight. Then I joined Steve in the tent. I put on my goosedown booties and wool cap, slipped into my bag, and read a biography of Andrew Jackson for a while before turning out the lantern and sleeping.

Sunlight had already struck the tent when I woke up. Immediately I checked the thermometer; it read seventeen degrees. Fully clothed, I emerged into the early sunlight. In appreciation of our warm fire the night before, one of the men from the other group already had a fire going. With the hot coffee, the fire, and the sunshine, I was as warm as could be hoped for on such a frozen Smoky Mountain morning.

Steve helped me take down the tent. We then devoured a quick breakfast of link sausages, scrambled eggs, and hot chocolate. After packing up, we bade farewell to the 'Bamans and headed back up to the Thomas Divide Trail. At the trail junction, we turned south on the trail named for Will Thomas, an adopted Cherokee chief, entrepreneur, and Confederate colonel who once wielded considerable influence over western North Carolina. Hiking primarily downhill for the next three miles, we came into Deeplow Gap (elevation 3,715 feet). Any traces of snow were left behind. We climbed out of the gap and tramped southward on Thomas Divide. The day had turned partly cloudy, but the temperature now was above freezing.

Off in the distance, occasional breaks in the leafless trees allowed views of the waves of mountains to the east, far into North Carolina. Five and a half miles from Newton Bald, the trail met and began to parallel the park's southern boundary. Within a mile, the narrow descending footpath suddenly turned and began following an old road. The trail-turned-road was more open, and the occasional sunny areas felt promising. After two miles on the road, we came to Stone Pile Gap and took a break. We ate a bite and drank the last of the water we had brought from Newton Bald.

Steve and I then left the ridge and veered west to Indian Creek, crossing several small branches (creeks), which made areas of the trail quite muddy. We followed a little side trail to Indian Creek Falls. The creek cascades twenty-five feet down slick rocks, to form a wide circular pool before joining Deep Creek a short way down. I took a few photographs. It was now one o'clock in the afternoon. We already had hiked almost ten miles. We had seen no one on the Thomas Divide Trail, but now, a tenth of a mile past Indian Creek Falls, we intersected the Deep Creek Trail. We entered an area of former settlement. Heading north, upstream, we began to see a few day hikers coming from the Deep Creek campground, which lay downstream about a mile.

At 2:30 we came to our campsite, Bumgardner Branch (elevation 2,160 feet). A carpet of hardwood leaves covered the creekside site. We both were relieved to shed our packs. The day was at its warmest, forty-one degrees. After downing a cup of coffee, I decided to fish. I assembled my rod, put a Roostertail on my line, and hit Deep Creek. Near the campsite, the creek was shallow and shoaly, not conducive to spinner-fishing, which is more productive in water with a series of plunge pools. After an hour of fishless casting and unwilling to put forth the effort to find suitable fishing waters, I returned to the campsite.

On the return trip, I noticed a white object partially buried in the ground. I dug around it with a stick, then with my fingers pulled it free from the soil. It was piece of broken plate, a sign of a dwelling. Settlers in the Deep Creek Valley lived in much the same fashion as other mountain folk. They lived in one-room cabins of rough-hewn lumber chinked with mud or moss to keep out the wind. A well-built fireplace stood at one end of the cabin, serving as both stove and heat source. The smell of wood smoke permeated these cabins from the floor to the loft above, where children often slept. The settlers' lives were filled with hardship, amid the resplendent scenery. Many lived and died knowing no other life, never having left the shadow of the Smokies, and are buried in obscure cemeteries deep in isolated coves in the mountains.

Steve was resting against a tree, enjoying a little sunshine while reading a book. I donned a sweater and set off to collect firewood. I found wood by scrambling up a steep hill near camp. Most people look in the most accessible locations first and end up with no wood. I go first to the least accessible spot and usually find plenty of dead wood. So I get more wood in less time. By five o'clock we had a nice fire going to complement our tomato-soup appetizer. I then concocted a pasta and cheese mash from a boxed mix. It tasted fine and stuck to our ribs.

At dusk, a noisy group of two men and a bunch of children paraded into the campsite. I offered my lantern to help them set up. One of the men wanted to put Coleman fuel in his kerosene lantern. I finally convinced him that this was not a good idea, because the two are incompatible and mixing them can cause an explosion. Somehow they found some wood in the dark, then kept pouring gas on the wood to get a fire going. For an hour, bright flashes of light leapt from their fire ring. I was sure somebody was going to get hurt. Fortunately, no one was. I got my lantern back at 9, three hours after it had been borrowed.

Apparently the children were too scared to sleep out in the woods, so the whole group stayed up by the fire for the duration of the night. Their noise kept me awake. No night is longer than one spent trapped in a sleeping bag on a chill wintry night, without sleep.

I arose next day to a sunny, twenty-five-degree morning. Steve was already awake and packed. He handed me a can of sardines before departing on his way up the Deep Creek Trail to Newfound Gap Road and then home to Knoxville. That was all right with me, because I planned to devote the day to catching fish. I drank several steaming cups of java to accompany my breakfast of fried sardines and eggs.

I packed and immediately began climbing a side ridge, staying on the east side of the creek. The frozen leaves crackled under foot as I hiked. I began climbing a series of side ridges, then descending down to the creek, instead of fording like they did on Deep Creek in the old days. I was happy not to be fording on this nippy morning. After passing two backcountry campsites, McCracken Branch and Nicks Nest Branch, I came to the renowned Bryson Place, site of a former hunting and fishing lodge and now a backcountry campsite three and a half miles from where I had started. A foundation is all that remains of the old building.

Another half-mile of riverside tramping brought me to the evening's campsite, Burnt Spruce. A flat area forested primarily with hemlock, it is just a thicket away from Deep Creek. No spruce trees actually grow here; the early settlers called hemlock "spruce." And the name stuck. The time was now 11 A.M. The sky had clouded over, but the temperature had risen to forty-five degrees. I could hardly wait to go fishing. I dropped my pack and hurriedly assembled my rod. Since it was cold, I would have to fish from the bank, hampering my ability to cover the creek while casting. But this far up, Deep Creek was small enough that it was possible to do a pretty fair job while making sure that I did not take an unintentional swim. I hung my pack on a high tree branch for security, then went upstream.

Ten minutes later I landed a pan-sized rainbow, which fueled my excitement. In the next pool, my Roostertail became hung on the creek bottom. My line broke as I tried to get it loose. That is a major disadvantage of not being willing to wade in the creek: you are going to lose more lures than usual. But I had been prepared for that. After attaching another lure, I caught two more trout and strung them on a stout stick running through their gills. Then I plunged the stick into the creek bank's edge just below the water line. Up at the confluence of Deep Creek and Nettle Creek, I cast into a slow pool near some jammed logs and landed a nice, hard-fighting brown trout. I put him in a tiny side pool of Nettle Creek.

Because of the cloud cover, I could not tell the time. But I knew I needed one more fish. And soon I had a rainbow, hooked on an orange Roostertail. I had caught my limit. I retrieved my fish and rushed back to camp.

Upon arrival at Burnt Spruce, I met two horsemen who had taken a break at the campsite and had made a small fire to warm up after their ride along Noland Divide. I told them that I would be glad to take over the fire. They obliged and in a short time went on their way. It was 3 P.M. I cleaned the fish, built up the fire, and got ready for the next phase of the day. Self-satisfied, I enjoyed the warmth of the fire in the dark mountains, reliving my day along the friendly stream and preparing to cook fresh-caught trout. I let one side of the fire die down and spread out the hot coals. On the coals I placed the trout—buttered, topped with chopped purple onion, and wrapped in foil. I cooked them ten minutes, turned them, and cooked them another five. In dying daylight, I dined on succulent fish complemented by brown rice. It was delectable.

After supper, I sat under my hanging lantern listening to the music of Deep Creek. In this watershed were born countless fishing tales, many of which centered around the famed angler of the first half of the twentieth century, Mark Cathey. The peerless Cathey, with the hardened face of a mountaineer, often drew an audience eager to watch his unusual fly-fishing techniques. Though he was not one to boast, his reputation spread nonetheless, drawing anglers from far away to try their hands in the streams of the Smokies. I have very far to go to match his fishing skills, but I feel a certain kinship with him and others who tramped along the banks of this history-steeped creek much the same today as it was in Cathey's day.

The cloud cover held in the heat, so the temperature was in the low forties. From the look of the sky, rain was imminent and probably would come by early morning. To facilitate a hasty early morning departure, I decided to risk getting wet by not putting up the tent. Around ten o'clock, I stretched out in my sleeping bag, with a plastic groundsheet beside me in case it rained. I folded my spare clothing into a makeshift pillow and went to sleep.

Just on the daylight side of dawn, I felt a slight pitter-patter on my face. The night before, I had placed my stove and a pot of water beside me, and I got the stove going in the murky half-light. Hoping for a short reprieve from a downpour, I quickly crammed my sleeping bag into its stuff sack, while raindrops tapped on the dry leaves. Warm drinks followed a quick morning meal, as the big raindrops turned to a light mist. I was on the move within thirty minutes of rising, marching up the Deep Creek Trail toward Newfound Gap Road.

Up the rocky creekside trail, a fog hung low over the valley. It was hard to tell if I was being rained on or if I was actually within the rain-bearing cloud; at any rate, I was getting wet. I started out cold but became warm heading upstream, my head hanging down as I climbed and the rain dripping down my nose. About three and a half miles up the trail, I came to Poke Patch campsite (elevation 3,000 feet). To this point, the grade mostly had been gentle. I continued hiking along the east side of Deep Creek for two and a half miles on an ever steeper trail that culminated in a series of demoralizing switchbacks just before arriving at Newfound Gap Road (elevation 4,810 feet). Along the way, a substantial drizzle fell. I was about two miles north of the Jeep. Soon I reached the road, then walked along its side to the Thomas Divide trailhead. I packed the vehicle, turned the heat on high, and headed home from my holiday in the Smokies.

Beyond the Road to Nowhere

Forty Miles near Fontana Lake

You need to get your feet wet sooner or later, but
you don't want to get in up to your ass in mud.
—John Barnhill

With Gatlinburg in the rearview mirror and darkness approaching, we motored up Newfound Gap Road toward the Tennessee–North Carolina border. Around noon, I had picked up my old college buddy, tall Steve Grayson, at his Knoxville apartment, for a Smoky Mountains backpacking expedition. He hails from West Virginia, so has a good appreciation of hilly terrain. We stopped at a grocery store in town for supplies, then Steve purchased a six-pack of beer and a pint of Tennessee whiskey. As the mid-December afternoon quickly passed, he sat back and sipped.

At the Sugarlands Visitors Center, the usual auto tourists milled around, wondering how best to enjoy the Smokies from the safety and warmth of their cars. As I was obtaining our backcountry camping permit, I heard an overweight flatlander, from somewhere north of the South, ask a park ranger, "What time do you feed the bears?" I chuckled, remembering with embarrassment my initial queries into the wonders of the Great Smoky Mountains National Park. After spending over five hundred nights, in addition to numerous day trips, backpacking in these majestic highlands, I continue to add to my knowledge about the intricate and complex web Mother Nature has woven here. By the time we reached Newfound Gap and began our descent into North Carolina, darkness had fallen.

In the dashboard-lit Jeep, the atmosphere was jovial as we recalled college antics and earlier camping trips. Steve was in a mood to celebrate. He had just completed another semester at the University of Tennessee, on the way to earning his second degree, in forestry. I looked forward to sharing in his newly acquired knowledge. We passed through the tourist town of Cherokee, North Carolina, and then Bryson City, county seat of mountainous Swain County. At about 7 P.M., we turned onto Northshore Road, just outside Bryson City, and into the blackness of the Smokies. Local Carolinians refer to Northshore Road as the "Road to Nowhere." In late 1941, impelled by World War II, construction of nearby Fontana Dam began. Slightly over two years later, in an engineering feat still considered amazing, the dam was complete. Much of Swain County—including thousands of acres of old homesites, roads, forests, and farmlands—was flooded, forming Fontana Lake. The waters of the lake, whose surface rests at an elevation of 1,710 feet, are held back by the highest dam east of the Rocky Mountains, 480 feet tall. The clear green lake holds a variety of fish, from bass and bream to trout and walleye. Nestled between the Smokies to the north and the Nantahala National Forest to the south, the scenery attracts a large number of visitors, including plenty of fishermen.

Some area residents experience the lake as a barrier separating them from their heritage. The offspring of pre-park residents are barred from living in the park, but their family plots remain there. Because of the flooding, many area settlers' gravesites, now within the national park's perimeters, no longer could be reached by auto. To appease the local citizens, the federal government agreed to build a road to reach these gravesites. The road was to follow the northern shore of Fontana Lake, cutting across several major watersheds. Several conservation groups opposed the road, eventually halting its construction. As a result, the road stops abruptly just beyond the Noland Creek watershed, a little more than seven miles beyond Bryson City.

Ecologically speaking, stopping construction of the road

was wise. Roads, especially those cutting through hills and ex-
posing rock, have a negative impact on water quality. Any un-
natural division in a wilderness threatens the flora and fauna
existing there. The threat to animals may come from being shot
with a poacher's high-powered rifle or accidentally being hit by
a car at night. Plants may be affected as thieves hunt ginseng
or rare wildflowers. Another threat is more subtle—the inva-
sion of exotic life via people and cars. The road is a boon to
those wanting a brief auto overview of the park's south side,
however. It allows those on foot or horseback to access trails off
the road and is especially helpful to people visiting their ances-
tors' graves. For the geologist, the rock exposure opens a window on the past, through which one can learn about the generally invisible subsurface of the Smokies.

On a small scale, the Northshore Road controversy epito-
mizes the conflict facing the entire Park Service: human access
versus wilderness preservation. Wilderness must be maintained
for the survival of Smoky Mountain plants and animals—that
is the mandate of the park. Yet we all own a piece of that park.
This fact makes it important for the Park Service to balance the
demands of people against the needs of the natural features of
the land. In this case, the wilderness "won," but, as human demands and natural needs change, the situation throughout the
park is far from static. For example, to facilitate the reintroduction of red wolves, the Thunderhead Prong watershed in the
Tremont area is currently closed to humans; as the animals get
acclimated to their new surroundings, they need minimal inter-
action with people.

As I drove along the "Road to Nowhere," a chill ran up my
spine as I thought of walking a flashlight-illuminated trail surrounded by dark forest. I am not much of a night hiker. I don't
feel as much a part of the woods when I can see only a few feet
in front of me. But nature is more than a visual show, as anyone
will attest who has heard the crash of Laurel Falls or smelled the
piney woods along Abrams Creek. Also, nature never sleeps. I
usually bed down out in the open and have had handfuls of
granddaddy longlegs crawl over my face on a summer night.
For other insects and for animals like the bobcat, nighttime is

the right time. In night hiking through the deep forest, I often get a creepy feeling like the one that comes over me while reading a scary book at home alone. I was not particularly worried about getting lost, as I had walked the trail before, but I did detect a minor slur in Steve's voice, and I wondered if he could hike all the way without mishap.

We loaded our packs in the glare of the Jeep's headlights. Steve and I each donned our AA-battery-powered headlamps and walked forward into the darkness. The temperature stood at forty-five degrees. About a hundred yards beyond the parking area at the end of Northshore Road, a large ridge seems to halt the progress of the abandoned road. One of the last tasks of the road crew was drilling a tunnel through that ridge. Thus, the trail includes a stroll of 150 yards through an unlit concrete tunnel leading to a dirt path. The crumbling asphalt stops just beyond the tunnel. For those leery of traversing the lonely shaft, the Park Service has created a trail around the ridge, which is now called Tunnel Ridge.

We took the tunnel. Its complete darkness initiated us to the evening's jaunt, as the sound of our footsteps echoed off the walls. After this strange beginning, the on-trail night hiking started. I led the way along the tapering, tree-canopied footpath, keeping my pace slower than usual, adjusting for the night walking. In fifteen minutes or so, we fell into the rhythm of our hike, laughing, talking, and making time. Suddenly I heard a thud behind me. Steve had taken a spill, stumbling over who knows what in the murky blackness, and had tumbled downhill. I swung around and shone my lantern upon his rumpled figure. Steve righted himself, adjusted his soiled pack, and laughed off his fall. He seemed to have felt no pain. He took a generous swig of whiskey from his canteen, and we proceeded.

After another half-hour of progress through the gloom, I heard the welcome sounds of Forney Creek, upon whose banks our campsite lay. We continued our descent without further misadventure, intersecting the Forney Creek Trail, two and a half miles from the trailhead. Steve and I continued our black march down the valley vehicle trail, illuminating and then crossing two wide, wooden bridges in a short distance. Shortly we reached our campsite, Lower Forney. The campsite usually sits on the shores of mountain-rimmed Fontana Lake, into which Forney Creek runs. In the late 1980s, drought caused Fontana's pool level to fall and remain far below its full pool elevation of 1,710 feet above sea level. Instead, Lower Forney sat at two hundred yards or more below its waterline. Now the lake level was even lower, as the Tennessee Valley Authority was doing repair work on the dam, drawing the lake level down still further to get the work done.

We dropped our packs in an open grassy area under a locust tree. In the glow of my Coleman lantern, I made a cup of hot chocolate as we pondered just how low the lake level was. I could hear Forney Creek splashing far down into the normally flooded valley. We concluded that the only way to find out for sure about the lake level was to walk down to the water. Strapping on our headlamps and leaving the lantern burning behind as a tiny beacon marking our camp, we walked away in pursuit of the creek sounds.

That was when I noticed the sky. Countless stars flickered over the lifeless lake bed. The Milky Way stretched across the heavens. It seemed that I could reach out and grasp any star of my choosing. I imagined the ancients beneath such a stellar lightshow, naming the constellations. Below our feet, the lake bed was dry and cracked but dotted with occasional mudholes, which we avoided. After twenty minutes of roving, we had not reached the lake yet, so we decided to backtrack to the campsite, with Forney roaring in the moonless distance.

Steve and I took separate return routes through the chilly, starry night, each guided by his headlamp. Suddenly, I heard a cry: "Help! Help!" Then there was a pause. "Help! Johnny, I'm not kidding." I looked over to my left and saw Steve thirty yards away, mired up to his knees in cold, thick mud. I spun his way and quickly found myself, too, in mud up to my boot-tops. I stopped and yelled, "I can't help; I'll only get stuck myself."

Instead, I adjusted my light onto his location. Then I realized his error. He had crossed an area of the lake bed where a small trickle of water enters through the woods, creating a frigid mudhole. Steve struggled desperately, furiously pumping his legs and flailing his arms, only to mire himself further. He was now rooted almost to the waist. He leaned forward, spreading his weight across the brown muck, slowly extricating himself with his hands. But then he made another big mistake. In a panicky frenzy to escape the quagmire, he stood up and attempted to walk out. With his weight now distributed only on his booted feet, he quickly sank again. Once more he pulled himself out by lying face-forward, spreading his weight, treading with his hands, and wriggling his legs free. This time he took no chances. He lay on his stomach and half-crawled and half-swam forty feet across the muddy lake bed. He reminded me of a sea turtle crawling up on the beach to lay its eggs.

Steve was free, but in the struggle he had lost his headlamp. His red jacket and Gore-Tex wind pants were completely soaked in wet mud. A spattering of muck clung to his prominent chin. The whole incident was one of the funniest things I had ever seen.

Steve and I retraced our steps to the dry lake bed, as we plodded back to the pinpoint of light that marked the campsite. Upon arrival, I set up a windbreak with our two small ground sheets, while Steve changed out of his heavy, mud-encrusted clothes and donned a dry T-shirt, sweater, and khakis. I then built a small fire as Steve straggled over to nearby Forney Creek and attempted to wash his sloppy duds. It was now nearly midnight. I set out our bedrolls while Steve tried to dry his mudless, soaking wet clothes over the smoky fire. Later he extinguished the lantern, while I slumbered through the frosty night under the stars.

We rose to a cloudy, forty-degree day. I prepared our breakfast—a heaping helping of pancakes awash in syrup and margarine. I then assembled my spinning rod for a few casts into Forney Creek. The air was even cooler on the creek, and a light drizzle began to fall. The precipitation made the creekside rocks even more slippery than they had been before, so I forsook the fishing rather than risk a December dunking.

A good night's sleep had left Steve ready for the challenge of the twenty-mile Lakeshore Trail, which I had hiked once before. Technically, the Lakeshore Trail in its entirety extends for over thirty-five miles, from Northshore Road all the way to Fontana Dam, using trails that go by other names (for example, Pinnacle Creek Trail, which happens to be the trail closest to Fontana Lake). But the Lakeshore Trail proper is the twenty-mile section linking Forney and Hazel creeks.

We departed Lower Forney campsite in a light rain, hoping that it would remain light or dissipate altogether. The day's journey began with an ascent out of the Forney Creek Valley. Steve and I were to discover a pattern that characterizes the Lakeshore Trail. After leaving the valley, we made it to the point of a ridge. Beyond the ridge top, we descended snakelike into the next creek valley, whose waters flowed down, perpendicular to our westward course. Our westward course paralleled the crest of the Smokies, lying to our north. The two of us continued on this pattern.

Two other basic trail designs are used in these mountains. One follows a water drainage up to a gap, and the other follows a ridge line. Speed hiker Steve, out of sight ahead, led the way. The pewter sky above alternately dispensed light mist and steady rain. We remained wet but stayed warm while moving continuously. After about two hours, we came to an area that obviously had once been settled. The winter-brown, leafless forest was sparser here, at an earlier stage of regrowth than adjacent areas. We spotted an old washtub, a mason jar, a rusty bucket; then we came upon a standing chimney of a type unusual in the Smokies, made of manufactured bricks instead of stones. A series of low walls, made of local stone, created the effect of terracing on the surrounding hillside. To top it off, a hundred yards down the trail sat a banged-up jalopy from the 1930s. It looked completely out of place, especially now that the lake had cut the area off from any road. But in pre-park days, the locale had been laced with roads, one of which we were using as our trail.

We inspected the area thoroughly and left all historical artifacts in their places, in compliance with park rules. Such relics should be left alone for all hikers to see, because they comprise an anthropological exhibit. The two of us rambled on down the Lakeshore Trail, grateful for a brief letup in the rain. The

A RELIC OF THE PAST. A hundred yards down the trail sat a beat-up jalopy from the 1930s. It looked completely out of place, especially now that the lake had cut the area off from any road.

winter woodlands afforded us occasional views of the drastically lowered lake, which I estimated to be down 175 feet. The barren brown lake bottom provided a bizarre and desolate contrast, lying between the healthy blue-green lake and the densely forested mountainsides along which we tramped.

In an hour we passed the first of five backcountry lakeside campsites, three of which lie within two miles along the trail. We had chosen the third, Hicks Branch campsite, for two reasons: we would make more distance on this day, and it would be the ninety-eighth backcountry campsite or shelter in the park at which I had stayed overnight.

Upon arrival, we ditched our packs and changed into dry clothes. I had a notion to fish the lake and was soon sliding down the steep, exposed lake bed to the lake proper. On the lake bed, an old mud-encrusted rock wall stood naked and meandered down into the lake itself. Normally this remnant of pre-park, pre-lake homesteaders stood submerged and invisible. Note the irony: to generate the power that helps maintain our modern lifestyle, we must consign part of our land to the water. We create a beautiful lake, but, in so doing, we bury our past. Many had lived entire lives in the now-immersed Little Tennessee Valley. I wondered what other historical remains lay beneath Fontana's waters and those of every other artificial lake. Was the tradeoff worth it?

As I stood at the lake's edge, the rain commenced again. Treading carefully while ascending the rain-slickened lake bed, I returned to camp to make sure everything was not getting too soaked. Back at camp, Steve was building a fire, and together we gathered the ample but wet wood. The burst of rain subsided as darkness fell. Any adventurer planning to spend time in the Smokies must be ready to spend time in the rain. I try to go about my business and not let rain alter my plans too much. Rain, especially the sporadic kind that we experienced, has a way of paralyzing you into not doing anything but watching for a sign of change. Avoid rain paralysis. Our time in the wild is short enough.

Steve and I both knew we had small ground sheets, four feet by five or so, but each of us had thought the other was bringing a tarpaulin. There is no substitute for preparation, especially when planning a foray at least a day's hike from civilization. This lesson was going to be learned the hard way; the rain was sure to return. We rigged a woefully inadequate shelter of our plastic sheets. I fetched and lit my lantern, then prepared our evening fare before settling in for the long night. Steve rustled up two green sticks, and we roasted hot dogs over the fire. Just as we began to munch, the sky fell. The rain came down in torrents, while we huddled under our pitiful refuge, battered by moisture from all sides.

After a seemingly interminable period, the rain slowed to a drizzle, and the temperature hovered around forty degrees. With a big day ahead of us and nothing else to do, we pulled out our sleeping bags and lay down, the feet of our bags protruding into the mist. Being six feet and three inches tall, Steve had it even worse than I did; he had to curl his legs up to stay halfway dry. Our sleep was fitful at best. A complete night's sleep is essential out in the woods. A sleepless night does nothing to prepare you physically or mentally for a demanding hike.

At daybreak we awoke, considering ourselves lucky that, throughout the night, the rain had stayed light, letting up altogether occasionally. I had remained dry inside my bag, except for mist-dampened hair. I revived the fire and began drying the outside of my bag while quaffing steaming cups of coffee and hot chocolate. Steve boiled eggs on his stove and quickly loaded his pack. Hard-boiled eggs on the trail, says my old friend Tom Wortham, are "no muss, no fuss, no taste." I agree.

Steve and I planned to rendezvous five miles up Hazel Creek at the Sugar Fork campsite. I decided to take an alternate route to reach our meeting point. My plan was to attempt an unmaintained trail shortcut to Hazel Creek. But Steve was going to follow the Lakeshore Trail to Hazel, then head north up the Hazel Creek Trail for five miles to Sugar Fork. Having more mileage to cover, Steve embarked into the gray, wet day.

I scrambled eggs and toasted bagels over the withering coals, carefully dousing the fire after breakfast. After packing my damp belongings, I forged westward along the Lakeshore Trail. Pines— white, Virginia, and short-leaf—dominated the trailside, as the path veered southward two miles from the campsite. The timberland stood quiet and stayed quiet, as I swung back westward and entered the next major watershed, where Pilkey Branch, full of rainwater, surged noisily down the valley.

I had decided that at this juncture I would leave the Lakeshore Trail and find an old road that I had seen on certain maps, paralleling Pilkey Branch. I hoped to follow it northwestward up and over Welch Ridge, through Deep Gap, and down into the Hazel Creek watershed, to intersect the Hazel Creek Trail about three miles south of our planned campsite. The road was easy to locate; the Park Service maintains it for a short distance to a small graveyard situated among several former homesites. To access these graves, the rangers float visitors and a Jeep on pontoon boats across Fontana Lake, disembark, and then drive to the gravesites. The Park Service provides this service as part of the compromise over Northshore Road.

After hiking up the road awhile and rock-hopping Pilkey

Creek twice, I dropped my pack and found the graveyard, which had only four plots that I could see. Bright-hued plastic flowers adorned the graves, hideously colorful and oddly out of place amid the muted winter woods. The area warranted further exploration, but after a snack I felt compelled to move on, because the day was short and I needed as much daylight as I could get, in case I got lost.

I subsequently made a false start in the confusing surroundings but again found the overgrown road, which led up through a rhododendron patch. On unmaintained trails, former homesites and settlements usually are the most open areas to go through. Yet, because they were settled, the terraced land and old side roads often leave the hiker without clear indications of which way to go. In forested areas, hikers stick to the path; because of the constant treading, the trail appears as a distinct mark on the land, easy to follow. Trails through open areas, however, are more difficult to discern because hikers spread out to explore and wander around, so the trail tends to grow up and meld into the landscape.

The road I followed steadily became steeper, smaller, and more difficult to follow. At an elevation of twenty-four hundred feet, the road changed its northward course and began climbing northwestward to Deep Gap, high on Welch Ridge. Nearing Deep Gap, I was surprised to encounter another homesite, on extremely sloping terrain, where the homesteader must have had an especially difficult existence. Some ancient, rusty farm implements lay scattered about. I picked up an old scythe. What a story it might tell!

I stopped and caught my breath at the gusty gap, swirling with mist (elevation 3,400 feet). Then I dropped down into the Hazel Creek watershed. I soon lost the road but followed a small spring branch westward, for I knew it would lead down to Hazel Creek. An hour later I reached the main creek from Deep Gap. The watershed was surprisingly open, having mostly young trees. Eventually, about halfway down the small rill, I found the road again. After negotiating a seemingly impenetrable rhododendron thicket, I stood still and silent, looking across the splashy, cold Hazel Creek.

The shortcut had gone fairly well, but now I had to ford the creek, a prospect especially daunting in mid-December. But having no other option, I shed my shoes and socks, put them in my pack, and determinedly waded across with the aid of a stout limb for balance. I dried my numb legs and feet, put my shoes back on, then continued quickly up the Hazel Creek Trail, trying to warm up on this dark day. While hiking along the trail, I understood why being out in this wet, cold weather weeds out the less hearty backpackers. On the surface, the prospect of spending three days and nights in a sodden mountain wilderness is distinctly unappealing. But how else can you hear the mantra of rain dripping from winter's barren branches onto fallen autumn leaves? Or see fog rising up a hillside above the dampened pathway? Of course, hiking in the rain has its down side as well. Sloshing through mud can be exhausting. Breaks are pointless unless shelter is available. Yet precipitation is a major factor making the Smokies what they are. This factor was the reason we had not seen a soul since we left the car and would not do so for the rest of the trip.

After another ninety minutes on the vehicle trail, I arrived at Sugar Fork campsite. I had hiked six hours off- and on-trail, taking my pack off only once. When I relinquished it for the day, I felt as if I were walking on air. With less than two hours before sundown, though, more work lay before me. After coming all that way, I decided that I had to fish famed Hazel Creek. It had been featured in many fishing magazines over the years. Rod in hand, I made my way to the creek. After a few casts, I had had no takers; I was tired, and it really was not fun. Rock-hopping was akin to dancing on ice boulders. But while I was on the creek, a lone shaft of sunlight sneaked through the clouds for about two seconds—all the sun we would see during the entire rainy outing.

I returned to Sugar Fork (elevation 2,160 feet) and a really fine campsite. It is located at the confluence of Sugar Fork and Hazel Creek, in a stand of tall, straight pines, whose needles carpet the upland site. A superb fishing base, the area is also steeped in tempting historical fare for the amateur archeologist. The Hazel Creek Valley had been heavily settled and eventu-

ally logged over. Road beds stretch off in all directions. Homesites
and homesteader relics, such as washtubs, lie all about its hollows.
The remains of an old brick structure lie within a hundred yards
of the campsite itself.

As I built a fire, Steve strolled in, smiling and looking none
the worse for wear after hiking seventeen miles. Long hikes are
his forte. I began to prepare supper in the twilight. First I made
a pot of rice, then added dry cream of chicken soup mix and
two cans of Sweet Sue chicken to create my chicken-rice surprise, which we devoured in that unrefined manner exhibited
only by hungry hikers and chain-gang inmates. After cleaning
up the mess, we reclined by the fire, moving only as we had to
while drying our clothes. If you must dry your clothes by the
fire, watch them diligently and turn them frequently to avoid
burning, for the clothes you have with you are irreplaceable in
the mountains.

I heard a rustling just beyond the light of our camp. It was
late in the year for a bear, and I wondered what could be making
the noise. I shone my flashlight that direction, and six roving eyes
reflected the light. Raccoons! The three vagabonds slunk about,
hunting tasty morsels to augment their diets. They obviously were
regulars at this camp, victims who had become addicted to tasty
human fare, having lost their wildness forever. Yelling and throw-
ing sticks, we forced them to retreat. No physical harm was intended or done; after all, we were transients, passing through their
domain.

The struggles of the day had left us exhausted. Steve and I
once again erected our wretched little shelter under a rhododendron thicket, hoping the added cover would help stave off
the rain. We got into our sleeping bags and soon fell fast asleep,
our packs beside us. At some point in the night, I was awakened by screeching so acute that my hair stood on end. Two
feet from me, a pair of raccoons were in my pack, fighting over
a sleeve of crackers and a jar of peanut butter. Both Steve and I
turned our lights on the varmints, yelling all the while, and they
ran off into the night. On top of this midnight raid, it was raining again. Then Steve saw a coon run off with his food bag. He

STEVE FORDING HAZEL CREEK. Within a fifth of a mile, we had to ford nippy Hazel Creek.

gave chase, and the thief gave up his booty. We fell back asleep, only to be startled awake again by the nosy ring-tailed "little people," as the Cherokee called them.

Between our evening visitors and the rain, that night was turning into pure misery. I could have tried to avoid the raccoon problem by properly hanging our food. But here it would have been fruitless, as these rascals already had beaten the best food-hanging systems. Raccoons are crafty: they open zippers, stuff sacks, and other storage gadgets. To thwart the critters in their quest for human food, the Park Service since has installed at Sugar Fork a steel cord encircled in plastic tubing and suspended between two trees. Apparently raccoons cannot secure a hold on the plastic-covered cords. Any animal, mice included, will gnaw through a tent, pack cloth, or stuff sack to get to your food. In addition to damaging camping gear and losing food, the experience tends to "humanize" that animal's eating habits. That is one more reason to hang your food.

After sleeping fitfully, I began to see that slumber was futile. Steve announced that the time was 5:25 A.M. I had had enough and rose, in a light drizzle. After a tooth-and-nail dog-fight, I finally got the fire going. My knees were black and muddy, while my lungs were shot from leaning into the fire ring and blowing the damp debris to create a spark. As light overtook us, I scoured the campsite, gathering all packages that the coons had scattered from our packs and burning all trash that could be completely burned. The little burglars surprisingly had not been able to unscrew the tight lid on my peanut butter jar, so they had chewed through the plastic and had their fill.

Steve and I packed up, doused the fire, and checked the campsite for overlooked trash. We set out up the wide Hazel Creek Trail, leaving the victorious and undoubtedly full raccoons behind. It was 8:15. After two fast-paced miles up the trail, we veered east on the four-mile Cold Spring Gap Trail. Within a short one-fifth of a mile, we had to ford nippy Hazel Creek. We did so, then forged up the trail to a sharp switchback leading to a series of fords across Cold Spring Branch. It got to the point where we almost were hiking right up the creek amid the dripping rhododendron, as the rain had caused the water to rise.

The trail turned steeper and the fog thickened, but we kept our resolve, heaving with every breath. I broke into a sweat, de-spite the cold, misty sprinkle, becoming soaked all over. The rocky path seemed much longer than four miles. The last stretch before Cold Spring Gap is notoriously steep, and we deserved our rest when we attained the gap, forty-seven hundred feet high on Welch Ridge. Upon the ridge, the fog was quite dense; the mist-enshrouded forest below was a lost netherworld. Trees appeared and disappeared in the billowing fog, which changed in density at the whim of the wind. Our visibility varied from as much as a hundred feet to as little as ten.

Steve and I pressed on half a mile further, to our next trail junction, the Bear Creek Trail, also known as the Jumpup Ridge Trail. It connects Welch Ridge with Forney Creek. Jumpup Ridge got its name because the second half of the trail is so steep that, when a hiker tops the ridge, it seems that he has "jumped up." We began the steep descent and were relieved to be off the ridgetop, with its high winds. In an hour we had reached an area known as Poplar Flats and took a much-needed break. Poplar

Flats is now officially a backcountry campsite. We ate the last of the food, swallowing it down with the cool water of Bear Creek. The chilly breeze cut into our wet clothing so we trod on, though somewhat fatigued, having made ten miles. We had five more to go.

During the final winding couple of miles of the Jumpup Ridge Trail, we crossed three wooden bridges, the last of which spanned the crashing Forney Creek. These bridges spared us more fording, and we were thankful for that, as the temperature continued to fall. We really poured on the steam the final two miles to the Jeep.

Steve and I ended our journey as we had begun it, by walking once again through the strange tunnel at the end of the Road to Nowhere.

Winter

February's Freezing Chill Dance

Newfound Gap to King's Branch

Heading up Newfound Gap Road from Gatlinburg, questions circled my head like gnats in summer. But this was not summer; it was February—the dead of winter in the Great Smoky Mountains. I wondered: Did I have enough supplies? What would the weather be like? Would I get lonely? Would I get lost? What would happen? This was my first solo backpacking trip in winter and, in my warm apartment in town, it had seemed like an exciting thing to do. But now the leaden sky, dropping snow flurries upon the peaks of the Smokies, made the venture seem like a journey into a dark abyss.

I really did not want to get out of the car, but how could I go home and look at myself in the mirror if I didn't? As I searched within for nerve to open the car door, I remembered my father often telling me as a child, "Son, you're tough as nails." Was I? The time had come to find out. My courage reappeared as I saw the sign marking the upper terminus of the Deep Creek Trail.

Unloading quickly before I backed out, I bid my ride goodbye. My newly acquired backbone melted as I headed down the trail. The Smokies in winter can be as lonely as they are beautiful, quiet, and dark, colored in subtle tones of gray and brown. The slight crunch of my boots on the ground reminded me that I would be alone, every step of the way. I continued downhill, losing the elevation I had gained by auto. At midday I arrived at Poke Patch, my intended campsite, four miles from the trailhead.

This place looked even more desolate than the trailside surroundings had. A lone fire ring broke the plane of frozen leaves. Stiff wind cut right through my clothes. The dark sky still spit snow. Noon seemed more like dusk at this point. More hiking appealed to me; at least I would warm up again. Though the Park Service permit was for this campsite, I decided to hike on. Surely the next campsite would be better than this one.

Deep Creek surged loud and cold nearby. The hemlocks and poplars towered around me as I headed toward Nettle Creek campsite. The bouncing motion of my descent etched the pack straps into my shoulders. But the winter chill spurred me on, as I considered the chores involved in making camp.

When I arrived at the campsite, after six miles bearing my heavy winter pack filled with extra clothes and food for six days, I was ready to stop. The first task was to make a fire. Having dropped my pack, I gathered dead and downed wood, in accord with park regulations. There is no need to chop live trees under any circumstance, if you look hard enough for other wood. Green wood burns poorly, anyway. Search in the least accessible locations, for they have the most wood. Good, fairly dry kindling can be found near the base of any evergreen tree. Crumpling up newspaper I had brought along, I drizzled such kindling over it and laid slightly larger twigs over the whole affair, allowing plenty of space between the twigs. Adequate oxygen is as essential for the life of a fire as it is for the life of a human. I lit the paper. As the fire grew, I fed it slowly, making sure not to smother it. Within thirty minutes, I sat by a cheery blaze, having laid in plenty of wood for a frigid evening.

In early February, nights in the woods begin before 5 P.M. and drag on until 7:30 A.M., so I needed to get prepared quickly. I opened a can of corned beef, sliced several pieces, and set them on a small portable grill I had placed over the glowing coals. After flipping the corned beef slices, I placed sliced cheese to melt on pumpernickel rolls for a treat that warmed my bones. By the time I finished my repast, the dense black night had enveloped me. The temperature was already well below freezing, so I retired to my tent. There I donned many socks, long johns, T-shirts, and that all-important winter accessory, a wool cap. Keeping your head warm helps keep your body warm. Reading by candlelight while lying in a sleeping bag and holding Edward Abbey's *Desert Solitaire* with a gloved hand is no mean feat. Eventually sleep overtook me, and I stayed snug in my sleeping bag, which was rated for comfort to ten degrees above zero.

The next day I awoke feeling confident and was heartened to see skies that were only partly cloudy. I ate the rest of the corned beef on bagels and swallowed it down with coffee. Then I broke camp. After hiking a little more than a mile down the trail, I crossed a wooden bridge over Deep Creek. There began the Pole Road Trail. I steadily climbed along Pole Road Creek, which is a fine trout stream. I crossed the creek for the last time two miles beyond Deep Creek. The trail led steeply a mile toward Upper Sassafras Gap on Noland Divide. The climb negated the chill air as I gained elevation.

At the gap, I began the slippery seven-hundred-foot descent in less than a mile's distance to the Bald Creek–Noland Creek junction. The sun felt almost warm, and the day's prospects looked good. About a mile down the Noland Creek Trail, I successfully negotiated one of four "wet" fords of Noland Creek. Farther down, I was not so lucky. I tried to cross part of the creek on a log, then rock-hop the rest of the way across. But while going from log to rock, I slipped into several inches of ice-cold water, drenching myself from my knees down to my secondhand army combat boots. But I regrouped and a while later, after an eight-mile day, I squished into the Jerry Flats campsite. Jerry Flats is an old homesite, just shy of three thousand feet in elevation. Young trees are covering over the site, but the flat open area beckons as a stopping point. Soon I had my boots and socks laid out in a pitiful attempt to dry them in the weak winter sun. I sat against a tree hungrily eating lunch, saving the trash to start a fire later.

With daylight and its scant warmth already fading, I started my fire, having collected wood from a decent supply. The subsequent blaze warmed not only me but also my boots and socks. In fact, the flames were so warm that they burned two socks, the toe of one boot, and the laces of the other—a costly mishap. This particular scene has been played over and over around thousands of campfires through the years.

After dinner I climbed into my bag and drifted off listening to the transistor radio I had brought along. I listened to Reverend McGehee, a fire-and-brimstone preacher who, with his mountain twang, sounds like he is coming to you from the hills nearby. In reality, he is recorded in California. He talked about being "washed in the blood."

The next day, I hesitated before emerging from my toasty shell. Outside, the cold, dark early morning fueled my sense of desolation. Apparently my first major solo hike was a success, judging by how lonely I felt. After a tasteless oatmeal breakfast, I moved on, hiking along Noland Creek to the Springhouse Branch Trail, which led up to Forney Ridge. Old homesites were evident a short way up the trail. Crumbling stone fences, rock piles, and cabin foundations stood as relics recalling the lives of the early settlers. Winters surely were treacherous for these pioneers, with their simple means. I, in contrast, was just passing through.

The trail led up and out of the valley. As I climbed, the wind became a virtual gale at Board Camp Gap (named for an old cabin, made from rough-hewn boards, that once stood there). A few yards further, I turned up on the Forney Ridge Trail toward Clingman's Dome. My plan was to find an old trail leading down to my designated campsite on Forney Creek.

As I climbed, patches of snow appeared occasionally. With the temperature hovering around twenty-five degrees and wind gusts up to thirty miles per hour, I trudged on to keep from freezing. With the depth and coverage of snow increasing with every step, I accepted the fact that finding the old trail was unlikely. Changing my plans, I tramped onward up Forney Ridge. The snow slowly infiltrated my boots, particularly through the burned areas. My feet were wet, my jeans frozen from the knees down. I began to worry. Lifting my legs up and over the snow was an exhausting drudgery.

I stumbled on in a trancelike state, afraid to stop for fear of freezing to death. To my horror, I soon realized that hypothermia was setting in. I was only two miles from the imagined security of Clingman's Dome Road, which was closed this time of year. In my state, with the snow so deep, just a couple of miles was a world away. Finally, after slowing to a pace of one

mile per hour, I arrived at an open field called Andrews Bald (elevation 5,800 feet). The wind was punishing here in the open.
Despite the deep snow, I had been able to track the trail so far. But now, in my confusion, with no trees lining the pathway, I was baffled as to which way to go. I decided to cross the field and head uphill, just to keep moving. As I crossed the bald, the sun emerged, revealing an awesome mountain view. Snow-topped peaks in jagged and wavy arrays reflected sunbeams in crystalline patterns. Lazy clouds hung between scattered ridges. I thought, "This day is too beautiful to die in." But in the Smokies death by hypothermia was (and always is) a very real possibility.

The drifts on the field were deep, almost waist high. Rushing forward, I fell face down in the crusty snow. Panting heavily, I felt the frozen whiteness sting my ears and melt in my nostrils. I wanted to stay down, to yield to exhaustion. In my mind I pictured people dying of hypothermia, huddled together in deep woods in the dark of night. Only this was daytime, and the sun shone. Why did I feel like giving up? My mental capacities were diminishing, but I made up my mind that I had to go on. Standing erect, I brushed the snow off my upper body and began to plow across the bald.

At the edge of the field, I thought I distinguished an opening in the trees that might be a trail. It was. Knowing that I was not lost cheered me, but I could not ignore the fact that I was nearing total exhaustion. At the intersection of Forney Creek and Forney Ridge Trails, a short yet interminable distance from Andrews Bald, I called it quits. I could not go any farther. I dropped my pack and slumped against the intersection's trail sign. My feet were two frozen stumps, but I really did not care. I just wanted to go to sleep. Then I considered how nice it would be to be warm.

That notion was all I needed for motivation. I would make my stand here on the trail. I cleared away most of the snow from an area the size of my tent. Then I stomped the remaining snow flat and erected the shelter. The fact that I was camping illegally was of no concern at this point. Making camp was a slow and cumbersome process, with my numb fingers and foggy brain seeming almost to work against me. I climbed into the tent and put on dry socks, long underwear, and dry shirts.

Then I got my camp stove going, melted some snow, and used it to make hot oatmeal and coffee.

Later I prepared a hot water bottle and slid it into my bag. My feet tingled as they thawed. I felt so snug inside my bag, with the hot food warming me from inside. As I warmed, my brain thawed as well, and I began to realize how dangerous my situation had been. A shudder swept through me, as I considered how I nearly had succumbed to the truly deadly cold. I turned on my little transistor and heard the correct time: only 2 P.M. The preceding five hours had seemed endless, and, now that I was secure, I again reflected on what had almost happened on my first big winter hike. Being alone means that all responsibility relies on your shoulders; you should conduct yourself accordingly. Later I slept. I stayed in the tent until the next morning—reading, eating, sleeping, and thinking.

The next morning dawned sunny and bitterly cold. After breakfast I began once again to trudge uphill through deep snow. On one step the snowy crust held my weight, but on the next three I would sink almost to my thighs. The going was extremely slow and tiring, but I managed to negotiate the mile and a half to the AT, just west of Clingman's Dome. Endless snowy waves of mountains against the blue skyline offered a view thoroughly at odds with the sense of drudgery I was experiencing. At one point I was using as a goal the distance from one tree to the next. I had reached the highest elevation of my journey (6,500 feet), and from here the going would be mostly downhill. Even though I was on the popular AT, the snowy path was unbroken by boot tracks. The spirit-breaking march through deep snow continued for another two miles, until I hit the Goshen Prong Trail and headed down into Tennessee.

As I lost elevation, the snow became thinner, though the temperature was still well below freezing. The trail eventually led to Fish Camp Prong and a ford. Remembering my earlier drenching, I dreaded this. As I rock-hopped across the noisy creek, I glanced up to find myself eyeball to antler with a deer at the creek's edge. I was so startled that I lost my balance and fell in the creek. I looked up, but the buck had vanished. I picked myself up and kept going the remaining mile to Camp Rock campsite (elevation 3,200 feet). Along the way, I crossed the stream again. But this time I just walked right through the water, as I was already wet and the day's trek was nearing its end. This was poor discipline on my part— it certainly is not a good idea to get soaked while winter hiking.

At Camp Rock I changed socks yet again, put on long johns and my heavy army-surplus coat, then gathered wood for a triumphant bonfire. At this point I cared little if I looked like a fool wearing a green overcoat, white underwear, and black, burned boots. This time I took more care not to burn my clothes as I dried them by the fire. A hearty spaghetti dinner raised my spirits, but the afternoon had turned forbidding, with pewter skies and high wind. I got into my tent and read. My exhaustion summoned sleep before long. I slept as if dead.

When I awoke at 7 A.M. on the fifth day, the sky was sunny and the temperature twenty degrees. I knew I did not have another death march ahead, because I would remain in the snowless lowlands. Better still, my friends Michelle Olsen and John Harv Sampley—both fellow hikers and old college friends— were meeting me at my next destination, King's Branch campsite. So I headed down Fish Camp Prong, where, sure enough, I encountered the Little River and another water ford. This time I took off my boots, socks, and pants and did the freezing chill dance across the slippery rocks without incident. My feet were numb once again. So I dressed and marched on to the Cucumber Gap Trail. I felt confident now, having survived two wet fords, deep snow, constant subfreezing temperatures, and disorientation. The mental and physical roller coaster of a hike had been a real character-builder.

Some four miles later, I was descending the last of a series of gaps along the Meigs Mountain Trail and heading down to King's Branch and my friends, who surely were loaded down with steaks and other tasty food and drink. They had a short two-mile hike from the Jakes Creek trailhead in Elkmont. As planned, Harv and Michelle were there waiting with a warm fire and smiles to match. While we feasted, I recounted the tale of my trip. Reliving the events in words reminded me of many lessons learned on my first solo winter trip. Then we retired. I had made it.

Wonder and Fellowship High in the Smokies

Kephart Prong to Greenbriar

There are no friendships like those that are made
under canvas and in the open field.

—Horace Kephart

It was almost dusk; my world was a hundred shades of gray. I
rushed downhill, stumbling over unseen rocks, the weight of
my heavy pack shifting haphazardly on my back. Limbs, brush,
and briars continually whipped my sweat-soaked face, obscur-
ing my path. What path? Which way to go? I did not know
which way to go! Somewhere in my throbbing head, a distant
hoarse voice pleaded, "Stop, get your bearings, calm down!" Yet
panic reigned. I plunged ahead.

Crashing down a ravine, I fell forward, tumbling into dense
rhododendron, its distinctive smell pervading my nostrils. While
I lay still, blood pushed from a jagged cut above my eye, while my
chest heaved, seeking air. I was more confused than ever. Which
way to go? I was absolutely lost—completely disoriented. My de-
spair was as thick as the woods around me.

Then I awoke. I had endured yet another hiking nightmare. While such a dream rarely haunts me in the city, a mountain phantasm like that fairly often plagues me in the woods.

Dream or no dream, I was alone high in the Smokies at
Kephart Prong, with rain falling on and around the shelter in
which I lay. The clock on my camera told me it was 4 P.M.
Through the chain-link fence fronting the enclosure, the after-

noon woods looked dark, wet, and lonely. The leafless trees in the misty fog stood like skeletons posing in evil shapes, while sodden brown leaves stained the ground in their journey to dust. The dream had left me feeling empty inside. A vague fear lurked, with no object that I could attach to it. I shrank into the warmth of my sleeping bag, shut my eyes, and lay still for a few more minutes, trying to shake the nightmare that lingered like a hangover.

I had begun my outing at the Kephart Prong trailhead, eight and a half miles into North Carolina on Newfound Gap Road, arriving at ten that morning. The cheerless rain that had begun the day before was persisting, as it so often does in the Great Smoky Mountains. Nonetheless, knowing that my destination was a dry shelter only two miles distant offered some comfort. It was pointless to wait out the storm. Stalled against the Appalachian Range, a late November cold front was likely to dump three or four inches of rain before moving on.

Thus I packed up, using my wet-weather loading mode. First I put my spare clothing into a plastic garbage bag, then put it into my pack. I put my sleeping bag, already in its water-resistant stuff sack, into another bag and strapped it to the bottom of my external frame pack. I also put my rolled up sleeping pad into a plastic bag. Today's packs, made mostly of coated Cordura nylon, are supposed to be waterproof. But wet clothing and a wet sleeping bag can be downright dangerous in cold weather. A waterproof pack cover is a good idea. It is a lot easier to keep dry items from getting wet than it is to get wet items dry in a late fall rain. A few minutes of forethought at home can save you hours of holding wet clothes over a smoky fire until your arms ache—assuming that you can get a fire going at all.

Having loaded up, I stepped out into the rain and immediately crossed the Oconaluftee River on a wide bridge. *Oconaluftee* actually means "by the river" (as was often the case, white settlers corrupted the Cherokee word in naming the river). Its headwaters originate near Newfound Gap and flow into the Tuckasegee River near Bryson City, North Carolina. Just beyond the bridge stood the remnants of an old Civilian Conservation Corps (CCC) camp. Stone foundations, a large fireplace, and a crumbling fish hatchery marked the spot where the camp once stood.

During the Great Depression of the 1930s, these CCC camps sprang up almost overnight all over the Smokies, employing young men who worked hard at improving the new national park. They constructed trails and built facilities for tourists. These camps were poorly managed, however; a lot of effort was wasted. Trails built by the CCC or those built by pioneers and later regraded were not maintained. But legacies of the camps remain. Those CCC workers became part of American history—and the history of the Smokies as well. As a matter of fact, campsite number 71 on Forney Creek bears the name CCC, for the camp that once stood there.

I headed west, making the first of four crossings of Kephart Prong, and made good time upstream. I find that I always quicken the pace when hiking in the rain. Still, I have to appreciate the precipitation, as without it the Smokies would not be the ecological wonderland they are. I was grateful that the narrow, shaved-timber foot logs spanning the creek had handrails, made of wood, because they were quite slippery. Even under dry conditions they are slick and often moss-covered, since they remain beneath the leafy forest canopy most of the year. Always use caution crossing these footbridges. On this occasion, I certainly did not want to slip into the turbulent, brush-shrouded trout stream in forty-degree rain.

I sloshed up the old railroad grade and soon was at the shelter, which was the site of an old logging camp. Unfortunately, modern "woodsmen" with backpacks had done a little logging of their own here. The area around the shelter was beaten down and picked clean of firewood. Campers are supposed to use only dead and downed wood for fires, but naked stumps of trees up to four inches in diameter offered mute testimony to blatant violation of this regulation.

This Park Service regulation is designed to protect the ecosystem as well as the scenery. Standing dead trees, for example, provide nesting sites for many birds; the trees also house insects that in turn are food for the birds. So it goes, up the food chain. The degraded conditions around the shelter made a good case for the Park Service's strategy of fixed campsites. If left free to camp where they pleased, certain thoughtless backpackers soon would ruin every inviting flat spot in the mountains. Many fixed campsites are in fine shape, however.

It was not surprising that I had the shelter (at an elevation of nearly four thousand feet) to myself on a rainy weekday. Backpacking is most popular on weekends, and a steady rain deters more than a few. Still wet, I fetched water from the prong. Upon my return I donned a dry chamois shirt and good down booties, then fired up some water for my powdered cider. The hot elixir failed to best the chill, so I fluffed my bag on the shelter bunk, slipped inside, and began to read the newspaper. I promptly fell asleep and dreamed of being lost.

After only an hour or two of sleep, I awoke with a mighty hunger. I drank an eye-opening cup of coffee and hustled up some wood. I scoured the area, picking up even the scrawniest twigs, until I had enough fuel for a cooking fire. The dancing flames added cheer to a dismal, ever-darkening late afternoon. When making a cooking fire, I use sticks no bigger around than my thumb. After raising the fire from infancy, I carefully stack broken sticks no longer than eighteen inches in a crisscross pattern an inch or two apart. This allows plenty of oxygen to get to the fire and helps build the coals for easier cooking. A three- or four-inch bed of coals will more than suffice to cook the average outdoor meal.

Sitting before the hearth on a seat of stone, poking the fire, and relishing its warmth, I built a coal bed, then opened a can of beans and set it at the fire's edge to heat. Later, I bridged the glowing coals with my grill and set two boneless chicken breasts upon it to cook. While they grilled, I sliced two large kaiser rolls and some cheddar cheese. After toasting the rolls, I made chicken sandwiches and beans; they warmed my belly and re-fueled me for the evening ahead. I was warm and content in the rainy and unforgiving valley of Kephart Prong.

Conscientiously I burned all my trash that would burn and bagged the rest. The fire, unreplenished, died slowly. The mercury in my thermometer registered just below forty degrees as I slid into my bag and read *Our Southern Highlanders* by Horace Kephart, for whom the shelter, creek, and a nearby mountain are named. The first edition of this book, about the people of

the Smoky Mountains and their ways, was published in 1913.
A native Midwesterner, Kephart came to the area searching for
the "back of beyond" and discovered a people left behind by
civilization and westward migration. The splendor of the region
captured his fancy, and he continued to study the region until
his death in 1931. By then he had become a major proponent
of the establishment of a national park in the Smokies.

One of the lures of the Smokies has always been that they
make history accessible. The mountains have reverted back to
a state similar to that faced by the first settlers of the "Land of
Blue Smoke." Most areas of original settlement in the eastern
United States have been bulldozed and covered over by the trap-
pings of modern man. But here, thanks to the foresight of some
of our forefathers, a hiker can walk the same creeks and hollows
that the pioneers did, finding an old dish, nails, or other relics
and seeing where the hand of man failed to conquer the mountain lands.

As I pondered Kephart's words, a noise startled me. I looked
up from my book, and in walked a skunk. I had carelessly left the
shelter gate open—but, crafty as the creatures are, it probably
would have made no difference. He sauntered through the shelter as if he owned the place. For all I know, he did. I lay still
and watched. He climbed on the bunk and over my bag. I was
not really scared of being sprayed; they have to feel threatened
first. I have learned to let them have the run of the campsite,
and eventually they wander off. Sure enough, about ten minutes later, he walked out of the gate. I shut the door behind him
and went to sleep.

I greeted the next morning late. The sky had cleared, and the
sun was rising over the mountainside. Still clad in long pants,
down booties, and wool cap, I put on a sweater, got out of the bag,
and started my ornery stove. I made no fire. Primed with coffee,
I sprang into action, packing my gear and wolfing down two
packages of cinnamon toaster pastries. I was ready to go about half
an hour after rising. At 9:30 A.M., I carefully crossed Kephart
Prong on a footbridge in front of the shelter. Soon the sun warmed
me, as I climbed northward on the Sweat Heifer Trail toward the
Tennessee–North Carolina state line and the AT.

Uptrail a mile, I began to follow an old railroad grade. The wide trail made for easy hiking, allowing me to ponder and appreciate the sun-streaked forest instead of watching where I put my feet. The woods were quiet, save for the rushing sounds of a nearby watercourse. The intonations of moving water are a constant in these highlands, except at the highest mountaintops. I wondered what it was like when a railroad steam engine chugged across this mountainside. The noise it must have made! That racket, combined with the sound of huge old-growth trees crashing to the ground and the din of all other facets of logging, surely saddened those who lived in the mountains as they saw the splendor turn into a wasteland of gullies and stumps.

Two miles beyond the shelter, the trail suddenly turned northeastward. Though I was nearly five thousand feet above sea level, the day was warm, as the sun dried the wet mountain slope. I shed my long-sleeved shirt. The trail soon left the grade and grew steep. In another mile, I came to a small spring seeping from a grassy knoll. Scattered across it were lichen-covered rocks, exhibiting their myriad shades of green. Both a fungus and algae, the lichen build soil by weathering rock through acid secretion. Here was a small world that alone could provide enough research material to occupy a curious botanist for years. I took a cool drink and a short rest, then climbed the final quarter-mile to the path's end (elevation 5,800 feet), where it met the AT.

Heading east on the AT, I gradually traversed the heavily forested Mount Kephart. A mile later, at the Boulevard Trail junction, I propped my pack against the trail sign and stopped for a rest. The pulsing sun brought the mercury to sixty-two degrees—weather unusual for November at six thousand feet. At the trail junction, I leaned back against my pack, absorbing rays and feeling very much a part of the wilderness. Less than twenty-four hours earlier, the dark, dripping forest had made me feel empty inside. But now, lightheaded with the elevation, the sun's glory, and the spruce-fir forest scenery, I was positively elated.

The woods give no quarter. They can offer a clear trout stream to fish or a blinding snowstorm in which to get lost. Always, what you see is what you get. As Horace Kephart wrote, "I love the wilderness because there are no shams in it."

After my inspiring break, I started along the Boulevard Trail, which forms a land bridge between Mount LeConte and the main crest of the Smokies. The name *Boulevard* might conjure up an image of a wide, flat trail crossing an expansive plain. However, the trail, five and a half miles long, is narrow and rocky, packed with precipitous drops and nasty climbs. It ends atop LeConte, third highest peak in the Smokies. The peak was named after Professor Joseph LeConte, who actually never saw his namesake. Princeton University geographer and geologist Arnold Guyot christened the peak in honor of his colleague LeConte. Guyot, who also has a Smoky mountain named after him, mapped and measured much of the Great Smoky Mountains in the 1850s.

Past Walker Camp Prong, coursing off Mount Kephart, the trail followed the snakelike ridge, offering views on either side and no comfort to those afraid of heights. Beyond Anakeesta Knob, to the west, a gray battalion of clouds stretching across the horizon marched toward me. I hurried through the scanty band of trees that clung to the forlorn ridgetop. Four miles beyond the AT, I made the lower reaches of LeConte. The trail turned east as I climbed up the slippery, pebble-strewn slope, which guarded long icicles melting above the trail. I re-entered cool, mossy woods beneath a canopy of evergreens, just before reaching a side trail that led to one of LeConte's famed views, Myrtle Point. A short way on, a large pile of flat stones marked the high point of Mount LeConte's 6,593 feet. I stopped, adding another stone to the marker. After descending to the Mount LeConte shelter, I thankfully took off my pack and went to the mountain's spring.

The spring lies just beyond the Mount LeConte Lodge. The lodge was built by a man named Jack Huff, who first operated it in the 1920s. It is composed of one main building, surrounded by a collection of what look like giant outhouses but really are individual guest cabins. Open from March to mid-November, this is the only lodge of its kind in the Smokies and is so popular that reservations must be made a year in advance. And the only way to get there is on foot.

While I was getting water, two fellow hikers walked up. An

amiable father and son from Indiana, they too were staying at the shelter, since the lodge was closed for the winter. I have run into many father-son combinations, but this one was special. The father was sixty-six years old, the son forty. They were toting full backpacks, and LeConte is a steep climb of five miles or more on any one of the six trails that ascend its slopes. The pair had made several pilgrimages to the Great Smoky Mountains, always backpacking. Their wilderness adventures had brought them closer together, they said.

The retired father, a slight man about 5'8" tall, had white hair but no stoop of the sort that often comes with age. His movements were swift and sure. Years of body maintenance had paid off. He also proudly let me know that he was an avid snow skier. Laughing to myself, I tried to imagine myself up here at sixty-six and hoped that I would be in good enough shape to make the climb. On many a sweaty, demoralizing, uphill climb, I have thought about the older man and the fortitude he had shown in trekking to the very top of LeConte with a full pack. His son showed signs of being an overworked desk slave. With a middle thicker than his father's, he tried to exercise as much as he could, but the demands of his business kept him tied up. But one look in his eyes convinced me that it was at times like these that he really felt alive.

We all returned to the shelter together. That same battalion of clouds surrounded the mountaintop as I brewed a cup of coffee. The sun was gone, the wind picked up, and the temperature dropped. I decided to walk to Myrtle Point. Standing on this rock outcropping was not for the faint of heart. The steady wind was strong enough to blow a sober sailor to his death. For this view into the heart of the Smokies, however, death perhaps was a risk worth taking. Out beyond the point, the overcast sky lent an unparalleled enormity to the steep, craggy, wooded ridges and their water-worn valleys, stretching off in all directions. They called out, daring one to cross them. No wonder the area became a backwater, settled—but never tamed—by a hardy few.

Back at the shelter, the father-son team cooked a potato-carrot stew, with fresh vegetables. They had plenty and offered me a bowl, which I gratefully devoured. While eating, we talked about our favorite spots in the Smokies. After supper I brewed a pot of coffee. We drank in a comfortable silence, biding our time until sunset.

Together we made our way to view the sunset on LeConte's western edge, at Cliff Top. The three of us sat beneath the back-lit cloud cover, wind chapping our faces and rushing past our ears. A deepening red aura rimmed the clouds to the west. We watched day become night. Ridge after ridge faded to the horizon. The tiny lights of Gatlinburg, Pigeon Forge, and all of East Tennessee twinkled in the darkening landscape. I thought with regret of all those people down below who had not seen, and might never see, a sight such as this. Then and there, I was experiencing *satori*—one of those lucid moments never to be forgotten.

The awesome splendor of Mount LeConte was a critical factor in the creation of the Great Smoky Mountains National Park. In the early 1920s, members of Congress responded to constituents' ongoing demands for a second national park east of the Mississippi River. Acadia National Park in Maine was the first, established in 1916. Other sites were being considered, but somewhere along the Appalachian Range seemed most work-able. A five-man committee was formed in 1924 by Secretary of the Interior Hubert Work to determine the next park's loca-tion. The group toured the Appalachian Mountains from north-ern Georgia to West Virginia. During this tour, a group of Knoxvillians escorted the committee to Mount LeConte. After seeing LeConte, the committee's report concluded, "The Great Smoky Mountains easily stand first because of the height of the mountains, depths of valleys, ruggedness of the area, and the unexampled variety of trees, shrubs, and plants." The Smokies won, but all Americans were the victors.

Inside the highest shelter in the park, perched at sixty-four hundred feet, the three of us sat mesmerized before the fire, each deep in his own thoughts. The temperature outside was forty degrees. Later the others went to sleep, vowing to awaken for the sunrise show at Myrtle Point. I asked them to wake me, though our chances of seeing the sun were slim. A creeping fog had enveloped the shelter; visibility was the length of my arm. After reading more of *Our Southern Highlanders,* I called it a night.

Before dawn, my shelter mates stirred. Outside the shelter—actually, drifting within the structure—was an impenetrable fog. My friends made the morning sojourn to the point, and I went back to sleep. It was fully day when they returned. "No view," muttered the father. I rekindled the fire and made a steamy cup of hot chocolate. The middle-aged son flapped some pancakes he made from scratch. Again he made more than they could eat, and I was the beneficiary of their bounty. Very tasty, but I forgot the recipe he recited.

What I really regret forgetting is their names. There is a special bond among hikers and backpackers, those who have lived the highs and lows of the trail and have seen the many sights alongside it. Since I met this pair, I have followed their example, befriending many I have encountered in the wilds. I have also made it a point to record vital information. Now I have many friends around this country who share a real appreciation of the outdoors.

The father-son team and I said our good-byes, and I left in the fog for Trillium Gap. Past the lodge, I found the rocky trail still soaked from the rains. I began a prolonged descent. In two miles I left behind the spruce-fir vegetation zone, as well as the fog. The high country has weather all its own. I shed my long pants and shirt, changing along with the changing microclimate. Below, framed by the leafless trees, Brushy Mountain stood spotlighted in the sun, while the trail remained in the shadow of massive Mount LeConte.

Eventually I reached Trillium Gap (elevation 4,700 feet), which lay three and a half miles from the shelter. It is so named for the profusion of flowers that bloom there in the spring. I dropped my pack and made the short climb to the top of tree-less Brushy Mountain. It is covered with thickets of mountain laurel, which the original settlers called "ivy." They also called rhododendron "laurel" and hemlock trees "spruce." Botanists of the last century, cataloging the vast array of plants in the Smokies, must have been confounded by all the names that the locals had given to their flora.

On top of Brushy, the wind blew strongly and steadily. Below was Gatlinburg. To the east lay the valley of Porters Creek, where I was heading. On the far side of the valley, Greenbriar Pinnacle, its swath of rock cutting diagonally near its crown, crowded the sky. Returning to Trillium Gap, I hoisted my pack and set off down the Brushy Mountain trail five miles to Greenbriar. The descent, continuous and pounding, led through several vegetation zones, from cove hardwoods to piney woods, and down to an area where a settlement formerly stood.

The young forest dated the settlement. The trees grew amid what now seemed haphazard stone fences leading off in all directions; these had been left by pre-park mountain farmers. At the time the park was being proposed, many homeowners were livid at the prospect of having to give up the soil they had cultivated. Others were happy to sell what really was marginal agricultural land, barely fit for farming. But, almost to a person, all felt an attachment to the special beauty of their mountain homeland, despite its meager yield.

Dried leaves swirled about me as I dropped off a side trail to Fittified Spring. I just had to drink from a spring by that name. After several mouthfuls of cool water, I hurried on, hoping it would not give me fits. I was looking forward to meeting hiking buddy Bob Davis at Porters Flat campsite, still five miles distant.

Bob and I had met years earlier through mutual friends and discovered that we both enjoyed the outdoor life. We decided to go backpacking together and soon were adventuring together frequently. Quiet, with a drooping mustache, he is a man of actions rather than words. In my early days on the trail, I would blaze down the path with no concern other than getting wherever I was going, in record time. A slow hiker who is always stopping to defog his glasses, Bob showed me how to slow down, look around, and observe the minute features of nature.

The wind grew stronger and the temperature rose as I made my way to Porters Flat. Having descended forty-five hundred feet in eight miles, I felt like I had been on a pogo stick with an anvil strapped to my back. One way to minimize this effect of downhill hiking is to cinch your pack's waist belt and shoulder and chest straps as tightly as possible without cutting off circulation to your arms. This lessens the bouncing motion of the pack as you descend. The three-mile grade up to Porters Flat would actually be a welcome change. That reminds me of Hiking Axiom No. 37: When hiking downhill, you sometimes wish you were hiking uphill; when hiking uphill, you always wish you were hiking downhill.

I turned up the foot trail that followed Porters Creek, which pounded and rustled, sounding like an autumn wind. In half a mile, after crossing the creek on a foot log, it was time for a break. When I took off my smelly T-shirt, the sixty-five-degree sunshine soothed my skin. I gobbled a quick bite to quiet my growling belly. The cool creek massaged my feet and restored my parched throat. After drowsing in the warm air, I forced myself up and replaced the load on my back. Sometimes I feel like an overworked pack mule.

I plodded up the valley with Porters Creek crashing through the valley on my right. The creek was barely visible, for practically the entire watershed floor is covered in one dense stand of dark green rhododendron, giving the area the luxuriant appearance of a rain forest, even when the deciduous trees have dropped their leaves. The humidity was that of a rain forest as well. The air was downright hot; I was sweating profusely. Once again on this trip, the weather had changed drastically. In little more than an hour, I arrived at the Porters Flat campsite (elevation 3,400 feet).

Bob was nowhere to be found. I was looking forward to his company, and it was already three o'clock. I went about setting up camp, feeling uneasy about Bob's absence and the threatening sky. Huge, dark clouds, black and swollen on their undersides, filled the sky; the wind blew strongly and erratically. The temperature had risen to seventy-five degrees. I turned on my transistor radio, listening for a forecast. Rain was on its way, and Knoxville already had a record high temperature for that date.

Then Bob walked up. Clad in his customary cut-off blue jeans, he was drenched in sweat. He muttered something about road repairs that required him to walk extra miles. He tossed aside his sopping, darkened shirt and drank heartily from his water bottle. A strong gust of air caught our attention. Warm winds seemed to blow in from all directions. Hemlocks and hardwoods swayed drunkenly, as we puttered about camp, catching each other up on our news. Around dusk the air stilled and cooled, as we ate supper. About 10 P.M., I put myself into my cocoon and hoped that the rain would hold off.

During the night, the loud and boisterous wind returned. At some point I woke up. Lying on my back, I observed the scene overhead. The moon lurked behind fast-moving clouds, lending them an eerie glow. The giants of the forest careened back and forth so wildly I thought they might crash and fall. Leaves blew helter-skelter about the campsite, leaving a dry, pungent scent in the air. Bob slept on, and eventually so did I.

At 8 A.M., we rose. Soon we were surging down the trail back to Greenbriar, anticipating the strong storm. Blackening clouds sped eastward over our neck of the woods, but we had just a short way to the end of the line, where Bob's car waited. Together, we made it out dry.

Over the Dome

A Winter Hike from Elkmont to Clingman's Dome

Courtesy of the Tennessee Valley Authority, heat was pumping through the vents in my house while I watched Knoxville's Channel Ten television weather forecaster Marti Skold deliver her chilling prediction: extreme bitter cold for the next five days, with temperatures twenty or more degrees below normal averages. My proposed hiking partner, John Cox, was watching the news, too. After conferring on the phone, we decided to go backpacking high in the Smokies anyway, citing the challenges of the cold and the solitude it would bring.

Our planned trek would take us from Elkmont, on the Tennessee side of the park near Gatlinburg, up and over Clingman's Dome (elevation 6,642 feet), where the weather was sure to be more severe than in the foothills near Knoxville. Then we would return to Elkmont by way of Sugarland Mountain. Before hanging up the phone, we vowed to be prepared for the extreme though not unprecedented harsh weather in the high country.

I carefully packed my clothing, making sure that the many layers I planned to wear would fit comfortably over one another, trying them on at home. Since we would be fording a river, I added a fourth pair of wool socks to the three pairs I normally take on winter trips. I brought two pairs of gloves, a thin polypropylene pair to be used for tasks requiring dexterity, and a thick wool pair for gathering wood and reading books. Fingers are the first body part to succumb to cold, not only from exposure to the elements, but from conduction while touching cold camping gear such as metal gas bottles, tarps, and cooking kits. A red wool cap for my head and leg gaiters to keep the snow out of my boots completed my winter ensemble. At the grocery store, we placed a heavy emphasis on mixes that yield soothing and warming hot liquids. Along with JFG Coffee, we bought hot chocolate, apple cider, and individual soup mixes.

An icy blast of air infiltrated my lungs, stopping my breath, at the end of Little River Road. Beyond our trailhead lay a winter wonderland. Two inches of virgin white snow covered the frozen ground; a layer of ice covered the rocks and slow-flowing areas on the clear blue Little River; while the long, green rhododendron leaves hung straight down, curled in their winter fashion, tightly as a cigar. Though it was noon, the sun shone only weakly, so we hurried as we loaded our packs. As this day was December 20, our trip was taking place during the shortest days of the year, forcing us to rush even more. We began marching up the icily shaded river gorge, needing no impetus other than the chill air, which registered eighteen degrees. Only movement kept us warm. Little did we know this was the warmest temperature we would experience for the next four days.

The walking was fairly easy over the crunching snow of the former logging road, and in a little over an hour we had covered the two miles to the Goshen Prong Trail intersection (elevation 2,700 feet). The snow gradually deepened as we gained elevation. The open, wide trail bore southwestward and led two hundred yards directly to the course of the Little River. The remnants of an old bridge clearly indicated how our predecessors had crossed the now-frigid waters. We had two choices: rock-hop or wade.

Rock-hopping is always a gamble. Often the surfaces of exposed rocks in mountain streams can be deceptively slippery. The unwieldy burden of a fully loaded backpack on one's back only complicates things. A wise hiker errs on the side of safety, because a miscalculation may result not only in a wet hiker and gear but a broken ankle or worse. An immobilizing injury in the Smokies can be deadly, especially in winter, with cold temperatures and, at times, solitude working against an injured person.

We chose to wade. Some hikers do it barefoot so as to keep footwear dry, but "barefootin'" it can result in injury, too. Most hikers ford streams with shoes on and socks off for maximum traction and minimum risk. I took off my shoes, socks, and pants; tied my laces together; and threw my shoes over my right shoulder. As I stood thus on the snow at the river's edge, pumping adrenaline impelled me into the icy water, and I gained balance even as the chill of the water stung me from feet to thighs. With the aid of a sturdy limb, I carefully and painfully worked my way across the rocky river bottom, as the rapids played noisily around me. After what seemed an eternity, I dropped my pack on the opposite bank. I dried myself with a small towel and changed back into my long pants, wool socks, and Vasque boots.

On the far bank John stood ready, shoeless in the wan winter sun, boots in hand, pants rolled above his knees, and lunged into the river. While negotiating the river, his balancing limb snapped. He slipped in, drenching his left side up to his chest. Despite the paralyzing chill of the water, he quickly righted himself and reached the river bank. I helped him get the slightly dampened pack off his back and extract some dry clothes. Somehow mercifully he had kept his boots dry. He placed his wet pants and shirt on the outside of his pack, vaguely hoping that they might dry.

We continued up the mountain-rimmed valley of Fish Camp Prong, slowly ascending into the very heart of the Smokies. On this winter day, the forest was quite sunny, its varied deciduous trees having relinquished their summer leaves. Just upstream from the junction with War Branch, Fish Camp Prong veered sharply to the right at the butt of a steep bluff. Down that bluff a small seep dripped, and the raw weather had changed the character of the bluff. A series of towering blue-white icicles had frozen together ten feet wide in places. Dropping forty or more feet, they formed a complex mosaic of fragile ice strongly clutching the bluff, much as winter now held this region in its grasp.

Rock outcrops are uncommon in these old mountains. Formed around 260 million years ago, the Smokies are a product of plate tectonics—the phenomena that occur when conti-

WINTER GRIPS THE SMOKIES. A series of towering blue-white icicles had frozen together ten feet wide in places. Dropping forty or more feet, they formed a complex mosaic of fragile ice strongly clutching the bluff, much as winter now held this region in its grasp.

nents crash into each other. The African and North American plates collided, uplifting the Appalachians; at least that is the prevailing theory. At the time, these mountains were much higher and rockier, not the forest-clothed peaks we see today. Billions upon billions of raindrops over millions of years slowly wore down the rock, building the soil upon which the complex life we see today could live and leaving little barren rock exposed.

After tramping another mile, we arrived at our first campsite, Camp Rock. Camp Rock looked a lot nicer in winter than it did in summer. The site had been overused and abused, so that portions had become barren and beaten down. But the clean, white snow concealed all that. The Park Service now wisely has relocated Camp Rock about half a mile up Fish Camp Prong, allowing the old site to recover from years of human impact.

John and I laid down our packs and began to set up camp. His wet clothes had not dried; they were frozen solid in twisted shapes—a cruel joke on one who challenges winter's reign in the Smokies. It was imperative that we make a fire for cooking, for warmth, and to thaw John's frozen garments. Firewood was scarce at the heavily used site, however, and the snow cover made it even harder to scare up wood on this short December day.

After finally gathering ample wood, John started the fire, while I fashioned a windbreak on one side of the fire ring, using a piece of plastic we had brought. Night soon descended, as did the temperature. Luckily, the stream was nearby; any water we stored was freezing in its container, rendering it useless.

We sipped coffee and hot chocolate by the fire, eventually getting cozy despite a thermometer reading of ten degrees. In winter backpacking, warmth is relative; between the windbreak and the fire, we felt warm. Beyond the windbreak, the cold was bitter. Around seven o'clock we roasted hot dogs over the pulsing fire, then smothering them in baked beans on toasted buns. As we enjoyed this delectable treat, we settled in close to the fire, swapping old hiking tales.

After the campfire camaraderie, we retired into our sleeping bags for the long winter night. Many backpackers would have thought us crazy for laying our foam pads and bags right on the snow. A good closed-cell foam pad insulates outdoor sleepers from what is under them surprisingly well. We knew we were going to be staying in shelters the following two nights and did not want to lug a tent. In general, I am not fond of tents—mainly because I am too lazy to carry them around, set them up, and then take them down. A tent closes me off from the outdoors, where I want to be. Tents certainly have a place, especially where insects can be bothersome, such as in the Florida Everglades or Minnesota's Great North Woods. In the Smokies, however, due to a lack of standing water and other factors, insect problems are usually mild, compared to other wilderness areas.

The morning sun rose to greet us, but it could not tempt us out of our bags. My feet were cold, despite being clad in three pairs of wool socks inside goosedown booties, inside my sleeping bag. We definitely were being challenged by the cold. The two of us had an undeclared contest to see who could be last to get out of his bag. The loser would have to revitalize the fire. I needed so badly to relieve myself that I finally lost. I got the fire going, and John, the winner, then rose and prepared breakfast. He set up my small, portable grill over the now-glowing coals and put some bacon on to fry. I lit the stove to cook some eggs, but when I tried to crack them, they were frozen solid. So I retrieved some water from Fish Camp Prong, put it on the stove, and placed the eggs in the warming water to thaw them out. It worked. We had our bacon, eggs, and toast.

I cleaned our dishes with snow. We repacked and began marching up Goshen Prong Trail. Within the first mile after leaving Camp Rock, we came across two more fords, much smaller than the ford of the day before. These were successfully crossed by rock-hopping. Shortly after the second ford, the trail tracked southward to follow Goshen Prong, at three thousand feet. The trail became steeper and the snow deeper, slowing our progress dramatically. But the sun-splashed day and bubbly Goshen Prong kept our spirits up. I stopped to inspect a small cave along the trail. Earlier I had noticed bear tracks. But they obviously were old, having partially melted and refrozen. I took off my pack and stupidly crawled into the small cave about eight feet before it became too cramped. It was dry but cold in there. No bear signs were evident.

The ascent began to sap my strength. Back along the trail, John was nowhere to be found. As the path attained Goshen Ridge, about forty-six hundred feet up, the snow was ten inches deep. Trudging in the endless snow, I had traveled only four miles, but it felt like ten. My spirits were sinking as deep as my boots were in the debilitating white powder. I stopped in a sunny spot and snacked. Off in the distance, the snowy white crown of Silers Bald stood tall and proud in the clear blue sky. My thermometer read fourteen degrees. A chill shot through my body, signaling me to move on. After a short, steep section, the trail began to level out. I thought I was on the brink of intersecting the AT, but I was mistaken. A couple miles of deep snow remained to be surmounted. In situations like this, I believe it is best just to keep plugging away, no matter how slowly I progress, and eventually I will get to where I want to be. And that is what finally happened.

Up on the main crest of the Smokies, the snow was at least a foot deep. The morning had turned into afternoon, and I was more than ready to get to the Double Springs Gap Trail shelter and drop my pack. I made the half-mile descent on the AT to the shelter (elevation 5,007 feet) as quickly as the snow would allow. The wind blew incessantly across the sunny clearing around the structure. I dragged into the three-sided dirt-floor shelter and cast down my pack. After resting a grand total of one minute, I realized that I would have to keep in motion to stay "warm." The outsides of my boots already were frozen stiff. I set out toward nearby Jenkins Knob and surprisingly found some wood; I stayed busy collecting and returning it to the shelter. With my foot I broke the dead wood into pieces that would fit into the small shelter fireplace. The thermometer, which I now checked frequently although I was at its mercy, registered three degrees.

About an hour after my arrival, I started the fire, but it took another twenty minutes before it put out any real heat in the bitter cold. John straggled up, just in time to enjoy the fruits of my labor. I left the shelter, located in Tennessee, and crossed the clearing into North Carolina, to one of the springs for which the gap is named. The water dripped slowly into my water bottle as the sun sank behind the trees in a grand show of colors, on this, the shortest day of the year. Soon we warmed ourselves with coffee and apple cider, drinking it beside the glowing fire. We praised ourselves for having purchased the warm liquids. With darkness fully around us, the cold became excessively biting. We hovered around the fire like moths around a candle. John and I kept on drinking the hot drinks as snow fell outside the shelter. We hoped against further snow accumulation. The snowy trails up here were deep enough.

John cooked up a pot of tuna helper, a filling, easy one-pot meal ideal for backpacking. We huddled close to the fire until nine o'clock, talking, tending the coals, and making periodic temperature checks. It was three degrees below zero just before we nestled into our sleeping bags. I heated a pot of water, put it in my water bottle, closed the lid tightly, wrapped it up in a thick shirt, and put it in the bottom of my sleeping bag for added warmth. I knew this night was going to be agony, for the temperature already was far below the ten-degree comfort rating of my bag. Moreover, the bag was five years old and had been through a lot, so the true comfort rating now was more like twenty-five to thirty degrees. But, probably due to the exhausting day, I fell asleep rather easily. Every task, no matter how simple, becomes time-consuming and arduous when backpacking in the depths of winter.

Later I awoke, chilled all over. My feet felt like ice blocks. The drawstring at the top of the bag was drawn tight, with a small opening for my mouth and nose. After this awakening I drifted in and out of sleep, occasionally peering out of my bag to check for the first sign of dawn's early light. John, in his bag that was comfort-rated for twenty degrees below zero, slept like a log.

Finally, an orange hue lined the eastern horizon, and I immediately was up and at the fireplace. The night before, I had placed some newspaper and kindling near the fireplace for quick morning fire ignition. My feet were grateful for the thawing heat. Steaming cups of hot chocolate and coffee also helped me get warm again. I do not know if our six remaining eggs ever thawed during the previous day, but again I dunked them in warm water before John fried them for our bacon-and-egg sandwiches on toasted English muffins.

DAWN AT DOUBLE SPRINGS GAP. Finally an orange hue lined the eastern horizon; immediately I was up and at the fireplace.

It was 9 A.M. before we started the grueling climb to Clingman's Dome. The woods changed to the spruce-fir forest that dominates the park's highest elevations. This particular area marks the southern extreme of this forest, which is more like those in Maine and southern Canada. The trailside evergreens drooped with the weight of the snow as we passed the six-thousand-foot elevation point. We looked out above the clouds, with only the highest ridges poking their heads up into the sun.

After a laborious three-mile climb along the AT, through ever-deepening snow, we arrived at the dome tower. The spot marks the highest point in Tennessee, in the Great Smoky Mountains National Park, and on the entire length of the two-thousand-mile AT. The wind cut us to the bone up on the tower. We briefly celebrated our 360-degree view with coffee from John's thermos and ate oatmeal cookies that were frozen solid. Our stay was brief; the bitter cold ran us off.

Earlier the Great Smoky Mountains had been much colder than this. At the beginning of the Ice Age, 1.8 million years ago, much of what is now the United States periodically was covered with glaciers. Though glaciers never reached the park, their influence on the land, its plants, and its animals was profound. Alpine plants grew above a tree line at five thousand feet. As the climate warmed, glaciers receded for the last time ten thousand years ago. The spruce-fir forest, which had migrated south during the cold period, took its place on the highest peaks. This is how northern flora and fauna got this far south. Now, these high mountaintops are, in effect, cool-climate "islands" upon which this life exists.

As the trail descended the north side of Clingman's Dome, John and I found ourselves slogging through drifts up to our waists. We kept moving just to stay warm, thrashing blindly, every now and then tumbling over snow-concealed rocks, not knowing what was under our feet. As the trail continued to straddle the Tennessee–North Carolina border, its exhausting up and down pathway was demoralizing. The sky was clouding; more snow would be disastrous. I was thankful when I saw the Mount Collins shelter's half-mile sign. It was off the AT, down Sugarland Mountain, which is really a linear ridge. The shelter is named for Robert Collins, a mountaineer of the mid-nineteenth century, who guided Arnold Guyot about the Smokies when he mapped these big mountains.

Upon arrival at the shelter, I immediately set about making a fire. Since this was a popular shelter, wood was fairly scarce; but my efforts were spurred on by the cold. I crumpled up the last of the newspaper we had brought along, then placed small, dry twigs over that. With a flick of my lighter I had a pyramid of heat. I continued to feed the fire.

My boots crunched through the otherwise silent snowy surroundings to the nearby spring, which was nearly frozen; the flow had been reduced to a slow drip. I stood bent over, contorted and freezing, holding the water bottle under the spring pipe, waiting for the bottle to fill. This was the Smoky Mountain version of Chinese water torture. When I returned from fetching water, John had arrived and was warming by the fire. In short order we drank hot apple cider, bracing for the challenge of another long, cold winter night at fifty-nine hundred feet on top of Old Smoky.

Darkness came quickly, but we were ready; we had laid in plenty of wood. The two of us then focused on filling our empty stomachs. We started with steamy cream of chicken soup. I then sautéed some rice and mixed it with canned chicken to complete our evening meal. I dreaded bedtime, because now it was colder than ever. Of course, in his toasty sleeping bag, John was not worried at all. I placed on my body every article of clothing I had brought and made a hot water bottle for good measure. I then stoked the fire just before I got into my bag, enhancing our chances for morning coals. I dozed off as I listened to the wind blow whistling through holes in the chinking of the stone shelter, not even wanting to consider the wind-chill factor. I made it through most of the night unconscious, but when I awoke darkness still prevailed and I was even colder than I had expected. Rubbing my heavily clad feet and squirming around helped little. I was having a nightmare awake. Getting the fire going crossed my mind, but I had no idea what time it was. Besides, as hellishly cold as I was in my bag, getting out of it seemed worse.

Daylight eventually—mercifully—came. Some coals remained in the fireplace, so a fire came easily. I knew it had been cold the night before, but when I got the water bottle out of my sleeping bag, I was shocked—the water in the bottle had partially frozen while in my bag!

The sun shone, and the coffee flowed, as John sluggishly got out of his warm haven to make pancakes. Our breakfast was eaten hurriedly before it became cold. We packed our gear one last time on this wickedly cold day. I kept my long johns on for the prolonged descent of Sugarland Mountain. My tortured feet were numb as we left the Mount Collins shelter for the hike of eight and a half miles to our next trail intersection.

The procession was slow, but the silence of the snowy woods, interrupted only by our footsteps on the blanket of snow, coupled with the views into the upper section of the Little River Valley, known as Elkmont, made it worthwhile. This "dismal gulf," as

famous Smokies old-timer Horace Kephart once called it, was
a shining winter panorama, with its frosted trees reflecting the
sunlight. It certainly deserved its protected national park status.

Four hours of continuous tramping through the isolated
timberland brought me to the Huskey Gap Trail, where the
pace picked up on a two-mile descent through second-growth
forest into the valley of the Little River. My feet remained cold
throughout the hike. Usually the movement of your feet inside
your boots will thaw cold feet, but not today. In an hour, as I
walked along the Little River, my thoughts dwelled on how
beautiful but cold the trip over Clingman's Dome had been.
Overall, it had been enjoyable, but at points it had seemed more
like a survival test.

When John arrived at the car shortly after me, the winter
shadows had grown long again. We tossed our packs in the car
and plopped into the seats. We had hiked thirteen and a half
miles through the snow that day, stopping only once. On the
way home, the two of us checked in at the Sugarlands visitors
center. There we found out that the temperature the night before
had gone down to thirteen degrees below zero at Newfound Gap,
almost a thousand feet lower than Mount Collins, where we had
been. John and I could not forget the deprivations we had just
suffered, but we felt satisfied that we not only had endured but
indeed had prevailed, in some of the harshest conditions this
region has to offer.

And Along Came the Front

Big Creek to Mount Sterling

The rain lashed us from all sides; wetness was everywhere in the air and in every other place on that mountaintop. Running splashily over the slushy snow patches, Bob and I rushed toward the crowded tent as if it were the gates of Heaven. Leaving our boots under the makeshift vestibule I had rigged with the tarp, we piled our wet coats on our packs and tried to find room to sit among all the camping gear strewn about on the tiny tent floor. Bob twisted and contorted himself as he began a vain attempt at organization. I knocked over an open water bottle with my feet, spilling its contents about. It was evident that we were in for a long one.

Thus began the eighteen-hour tent marathon. With two grown men, two full packs, and assorted gear in the tent, the situation was cramped at best. I stretched out my sleeping bag, slid in and attempted to get comfortable. At least we were out of the torrential downpour outside. Bob and I read, tried to doze, listened to the storm howl, talked, and counted the minutes and then the hours. I continually shifted positions in an attempt to get comfortable, wriggling around like a Mexican jumping bean. Knowing that I was tentbound precluded any chance of sleep. It was afternoon, anyway, and I had gotten more than my share of rest the night before. We were miles from anyone, trapped in a tiny shelter by a major storm. Such is the changing character of weather in the Smoky Mountains.

The Smokies themselves had undergone major changes during the preceding two hundred years. After 260 million years of slow change, followed by about ten thousand years in a reasonably stable state, the last two centuries—the blink of an eye, geologically speaking—had been virtually cataclysmic. A wave of change—a front, if you will—blew through the Smokies. First came the white man, settling and clearing the valleys. The real rainmakers, however, were his inventions: the band saw, splash dams, and the railroad, which extracted millions of board feet of timber before it was all over. Next, devastating fires and floods wracked the remnants of land the loggers had left behind. Now the Smokies have entered an era of recovery and restoration. Protection and reintroduction are the key concepts followed within the boundaries of the national park.

The tentathon continued into the dark of night. Around 7:30, we grew hungry. I unzipped the tent door and set up my stove in the vestibule, sheltered from the deluge. I brewed coffee and heated up canned beef stew. A portable camp stove really comes in handy in such dismal weather. We ate the filling slop, then continued the cycle of reading, flopping around, and talking from the warm cocoons of our sleeping bags. Bob's cynical analysis of our plight had me in stitches at times. The storm continued raging outside. I actually was afraid that a mighty gust of the fierce wind would blow down the tent. Around midnight I blew out the candle lantern and lay in my bag, thinking about how we had gotten where we were, until the wind finally lulled me to sleep.

Bob and I had begun our adventure at the Big Creek trailhead, whose watershed lies just over the North Carolina border from Tennessee, in the northeastern corner of the Smoky Mountains. This remote and rugged area, logged unmercifully in the early part of this century, once was barren but now is reforested. Ironically, the renewed beauty of the area is making it too popular for its own good.

When Bob Davis and I came to the area for a loop hike during the month of January, we had hoped to have the whole area to ourselves. The weather was forecast to be rainy, cold, and generally nasty. Much to our surprise, though, the day was sunny and fifty-five degrees as we left Bob's truck at the Big Creek ranger station and headed up the five-and-a-half-mile Big Creek Trail. This valley had been thoroughly traversed over the last hundred years. A railroad once had coursed along Big Creek, and a regular settlement had existed along the creek's lower reaches until the area was completely logged back in the 1920s and then abandoned by the Crestmont Lumber Company. World War I, followed by postwar reconstruction, spurred the demand for wood.

For anywhere from sixty-five cents to a dollar a day, loggers risked their lives from dusk to dawn, living in shacks that could be moved by rail or even living in rail cars themselves. A company store, where the employees could get goods on credit, often was located nearby, sometimes also in a rail car. Dances were organized on Saturday nights, and Sunday, the day of rest, centered around church, in the same building where the dance had been held the night before.

In my early days of backpacking in the Smokies, I resented the fact that human interventions had affected the landscape so much. I came to the national park to find pristine, virgin wilderness. As time went on, I began to appreciate the hardships and labor entailed in the pioneers' efforts to tame the rugged mountain landscape. Before, finding an old rusty washtub would negatively affect my experience in the wilds. Now I consider it a pleasant discovery when I spot a square, level parcel of land, grown up with young trees but subtly revealing the previous existence of human occupants. It adds an archeological element to a Smokies backpacking trip.

I also began to appreciate two other things. The creation of national parks in the West tended simply to involve claiming and designating the land as the park. In the case of the Great Smoky Mountains National Park, however, over sixty-five hundred separate tracts of land had to be purchased. National, state, local, and private funds were used to purchase tracts. Many owners, especially large lumber companies, fought over the selling prices, which eventually were negotiated through the courts. It

BOB AND I RELAX ALONG BIG CREEK. I took off my shirt as we basked in the sun.

was very difficult to do all this and to convince many angry landowners that the park was in the nation's best interest. What foresight that was!

Second, after one learns about the loggers' wanton destruction of the land and water of the Smokies, it is endlessly amazing to witness the recuperative powers of this resilient landscape. Although the land does not yet approach its old-growth state, it is vastly improved over its condition immediately after the logging era. As Bob and I began our trip, I looked forward to seeing, in the area we were about to traverse, both the natural features and those affected by human interventions.

We enjoyed the sunny day as we ambled up the gentle road and came upon a natural rock formation known as the Rock House. It is one of those rare natural shelters so predominant in the movies. During the logging days, laborers and their families stayed here until they found a place to live. As we investigated the Rock House, the smell of dry leaves permeated the balmy air. I even took off my shirt as we basked in the sun.

Just down the trail, at the two-mile mark, sun-splashed rhododendron lined Mouse Creek Falls, which tumbled down among mossy rocks. I took advantage of the photo opportunity by positioning myself at the base of the small falls and shooting upward.

The day was simply glorious, as warm as any January day can be in those mountains. The sky was so clear that it seemed we could reach out and touch the surrounding ridges. The trail climbed almost imperceptibly—no huffing, puffing, and having to watch our steps—so we could observe the splendor of the Big Creek Valley.

Colorful names dot the map of the Smokies, and we soon came across one of my personal favorites: Brakeshoe Spring. It got its name when a brakeshoe from a train was put there during the logging days by a thirsty engineer who liked to stop there for a drink. We followed his lead. Three hours from the truck, we crossed a bridge to the Walnut Bottoms. This backcountry camp-site is the busiest in the park. More campers and horsemen stay here than at any other backcountry area. Two camping sites, accommodating thirty-two people, are situated in the valley where Swallow Fork and Gunter Fork intersect Big Creek. One is a horse camp, and the other is for travelers on foot.

With all these people converging on one area, there is plenty of food, and the word is out among the bears. Without a doubt, Walnut Bottoms is the single worst area for problem bears, who persistently lurk in wait for any opportunity to pil-fer a backpacker's food. Campers are advised not to leave their packs on the ground even for short periods of time. To facili-tate safe food storage, the Park Service has erected tall poles with large hooks at the tops. The contraptions look like giant hat and coat racks. The idea is to hang one's backpack on the hooks. But the bears figured out how to shinny up the poles to get their treats. The Park Service once greased these poles. It is hard to get a heavy pack up there. A smaller pole with a hook on it is used to lift the pack onto the "hat rack." Quite a pro-cess, but well worth the effort, considering the damage that a bear can do to one's camping gear. Due to increasing bear problems, the Park Service now has installed bear-proof boxes on the ground. A backpacker puts food in them and shuts them securely with a critter-proof lock.

Upon arrival, we immediately went on bear alert. I set up my small so-called two-person tent, for we were expecting the skies to darken at any moment. I also erected an awning over the tent door with a tarp that Bob had brought along. As we worked on our camp chores, we were extra wary of any suspicious crackling of leaves. Mr. Bear surely was around.

Years earlier, I had come to Walnut Bottoms alone on a summer trip. I thought it a wise idea to befriend two men who were camped nearby. That night, three bears circled the edge of the circle of firelight. Their eyes reflected the beam of my flashlight, which I continually trained on them until the batteries went dead. I ended up staying awake all night by the fire, quaking in fear, as the men snored loudly in their tent fifteen feet away. What a greenhorn I was! I did not realize that the bears wanted my food, not my flank. Those men must have had some laughs on me.

This time, with Bob's low-key manner, greater experience, and level head, I managed to enjoy the waning minutes of the day. By sundown, we had a warm fire and plenty of wood. Neither other campers nor hungry bears had visited our campsite. We congratulated ourselves on being smart enough to come here during a weekday in winter, thereby avoiding other campers and reducing the chances of a bear encounter, as this was the bears' hibernation period. It has been found that bears of the Smokies usually den in hollow trees, often ninety or more feet above ground. They do not sleep continually during winter, but sometimes come out on warm, sunny days. Also, females den earlier than males.

Our two tiny candle lanterns barely lit the campsite as Bob placed our double-foil-wrapped potatoes in the glowing embers of the fire. After thirty minutes, I turned the spuds and placed my small grill on the left side of the fire, keeping a small amount of wood blazing on the right side, helping us to keep warm, for the temperature was just below forty degrees.

In half an hour, upon our reinforced paper plates sat the

quintessential manly outdoor meal: big, juicy steaks, buttery baked potatoes, and thick slices of garlic-spiced Texas toast. Our sumptuous repast, delicious as it was, acted as a veritable bear magnet. After dinner, as I lay staring drowsily into the fire, Bob reminded me to hang our packs. We covered our packs with garbage bags, still anticipating rain, and carefully hung them on the "hat rack." This completed, we retired to the tent, reading by candlelight until sleep overtook us.

I opened my eyes in the dim morning light of the tent, snug in my bag. All was quiet outside, although I had expected to wake up to the pitter-patter of rain. I unzipped the door and looked out. The sun shone on the top of the ridge. A chill hung in the shaded valley floor, as I layered on a sweater, wind jacket, and wool cap to get out into the morning and revive the fire. After quickly restarting the fire, I engaged in my customary morning coffee orgy. Bob soon crawled out of the tent, also surprised by the morning sun. I handed him a cup of joe as he rubbed his sleepy eyes. We took our unharmed packs from the poles. Bob then set about conjuring up a tasty breakfast nosh. He grilled boneless pork chops while scrambling eggs on the camp stove. I helped by making toast. We ate our breakfast in the hemlock-filtered sun, beside the ebbing fire. After eating, Bob doused the fire while I dismantled and packed the tent. I chose to wear shorts on the steep climb up the Swallow Fork Trail, feeling that my energy expenditure would keep me warm, although the temperature of Walnut Bottoms (elevation three thousand feet) was now in the mid-forties.

We retraced our steps over the bridge spanning Big Creek and to the Swallow Fork Trail junction, and began climbing southward toward Pretty Hollow Gap. At the four-thousand-foot level, small patches of lingering snow appeared. By the time we reached a sharp switchback three miles from Walnut Bottoms, the slope we were climbing was almost completely snow-covered.

I arrived at Pretty Hollow Gap (elevation 5,179 feet) first. The open area was free of snow, due to the angle and amount of sunlight it had received. We ourselves received no more sunlight, however, because along came the front we had been expecting. The sky crowded menacingly. A layer of blackness lay close to the ridgetop. I changed into long pants and flannel shirt while waiting for Bob to arrive. Bob hikes a little more slowly, stopping to enjoy the scenery. He soon walked up, dropped his pack, and announced that it was time for a little snack. We ate at the windswept gap. The biting wind cut short our break, leading me to wonder what the weather would be like on top of open Mount Sterling (elevation 5,842 feet), our intended destination. The temperature hovered in the mid-thirties as we began the two-mile uphill ascent along Mount Sterling Ridge. We soon entered the Canadian-type forest that cloaks only the loftiest areas of the Smokies. The wind howled unabated. I wondered why we had left the relative calm in the valley for this harsh ridge line. It must have been Bob's idea.

Two miles later, we were at Mount Sterling campsite, the highest backcountry campsite in the park without a shelter. Atop the mountain sits a fire tower, one of the last three old-fashioned metal towers left in the Smokies. At one time, tower sitters all over the park watched for fire, but nowadays fire watching is done by air. Most of the towers have been dismantled to eliminate maintenance costs and reduce the risk of injury to visitors. The other two metal towers are at Cove Mountain and Shuckstack Mountain.

At camp I was grateful to have the small tent, which Bob and I, as our first task, put up. The leaden sky spelled rain, and it was only a matter of time before it came down. I then made the steep half-mile trek down to the nearest spring and fetched water. Bob concluded that a fire was out of the question, and I concurred. The wind was high, and by the time we had the fire going, the rain was sure to be upon us.

We made the obligatory climb up the Mount Sterling fire tower. Up there, the wind was blowing horizontally and was so strong that I feared being blown off. The view beyond defined gloom. The sky could not have been darker during daytime, barring an eclipse. The black, wooded ridges were clouded in dark gray desolation. The tops of the red spruce trees swayed in the wind. I peered down toward our campsite. The tent stood forlorn on the snow-splotched ground. Such a lonesome-looking place! Raindrops began pelting my face, then fell harder.

The two of us descended the tower steps carefully. Once on the ground, we bolted for the tent, not considering our fate once we got inside. This was the worst weather in which to be camping—high wind, heavy rain, and a temperature just above freezing. The abysmal weather was ideal only for hypothermia. But we were in no real danger—except from tent-induced cabin fever.

We awoke at 8:30 A.M. I immediately unzipped the tent door to confirm with my eyes what my ears had already told me: the storm persisted, now more frenzied than ever. The weather certainly was not inviting, but the prospect of continuing our tossing, turning tent sentence was the worst of our options. We began to stir. Under the vestibule, Bob rustled up a breakfast of grits mixed with canned bacon bits, and oatmeal, all washed down with coffee and cocoa.

Inside the tent, we loaded our packs and donned our rain jackets. Then we ventured onto the foggy, rainy, windswept mountaintop. I quickly dismantled the tent, crammed it in its stuff sack, and lashed it onto my pack. Our escape route was the Baxter Creek Trail, a trail that has one of the most dramatic elevation changes from beginning to end—4,100 feet—in all the park.

Through the fog and mist we tramped, leaving the balsam forest a mile and a half from the tower. The weather had calmed, though much of the trail was covered with snow. Shortly, we left Mount Sterling Ridge. The rain eased. Though it was all downhill, the final six miles seemed longer. I guess I was just ready to get home. We had seen extreme changes in the weather, not unlike the changes the loggers brought to the forests of the Smokies. Originally, the mountains had been a study in quiet, beautiful serenity. Then came the dark and stormy period of the logger. But with protected status and time, the park is learning to shine again.

Spring

Everybody Loves Trout

Canoeing on Abrams Creek: Abrams Creek Ranger Station to Chilhowee Lake

I did not know how long the trip would be. I felt sure that the journey had been made before, though I had not seen it described in any guidebooks to the Great Smoky Mountains. Nor had I heard of anyone doing it. I had seen all of the route from a hiker's perspective. But on this day I would pursue an ambition of long standing: to canoe Abrams Creek, from the Abrams Creek Ranger Station down to Chilhowee Lake.

At the Map Store in Knoxville, I had obtained a United States Government Survey quadrangle map—a useful, detailed, large-scale map—showing the lower Abrams Creek area. The map had helped me pick out the junction of Shootly Branch and Abrams Creek as the site where my old friend and canoeing partner, Francisco Meyer, and I would spend the evening. Cisco is an outdoors enthusiast who has dabbled in everything from whitewater rafting to fly-fishing. I felt confident of his capabilities, despite his slight, thin frame—actually an advantage, since he would be in the front of the canoe, where, ideally, the lighter person sits. Cisco's river-reading experience would be needed to help us negotiate the creek.

Cisco and I were not worried about getting lost, because we planned to follow Abrams Creek from its known beginning to its known end. It was the unfamiliar rapids in between that might be troublesome. A small, twisting creek such as Abrams can be problematical on your first voyage down it, because you cannot see very far ahead. This makes it hard to position yourself correctly to run the roughest sections of water.

Since we were traveling by canoe and so had more room than usual for supplies, we indulged in special fare for the trip. Into the luxury of the ice chest we packed cokes, steaks, slaw, fruit, and other perishables that would have been left out had we been toting our food on our backs. Folding chairs and a small portable grill completed the deluxe camping package.

We left Knoxville in two vehicles. I left my Jeep at Chilhowee Lake, near Foothills Parkway, the endpoint of the trip. We then both rode in Cisco's truck to our starting point at the Abrams Creek ranger station. We carefully loaded the canoe with our food and gear, which included sleeping bags, sleeping pads, and fishing rods and tackle. The creek was up half a foot above its normal level, which I read as a good sign. I knew that there were trouble spots downstream where the water is usually very shallow. The extra water volume would allow us to pass more easily. I later was proved right, but the extra flow also made the river more "pushy"—that is, the current controlled our speed more than we liked.

At 3 P.M. we paddled off. The early May sun pierced the river birches and the elms lining the creek and glinted off the clear, cold water as we passed under a narrow footbridge. The bridge spanning the creek was part of the Rabbit Creek Trail, which leads to Cades Cove. The clarity of the water made the stream look shallower than it really was. We could see colored rocks on the creek bottom. These gentle initial shoals enhanced our confidence, and we floated slowly and easily, the loaded canoe lying low and heavy in the water.

About an hour into the trip, Cisco spotted a rare mountain clearing on the bank to our right. We pulled over to check it out. A hundred feet from the forested creek bank, we came to the remnants of a large field, still open in the center. The field proved to be a former homesite, as we spotted a chimney near the rear of the clearing, away from the watercourse. Along its edges, the opening slowly was being reclaimed by young trees such as sassafras and black walnut, both of which like to populate old fields and other disturbed sites at low elevations. Now, instead of nurturing corn and other vegetables, the field was a flourishing wildflower garden splashed in shades of purple, yellow, and red. Budding box-elder and other trees leaned over the river, fighting for sun and space, enclosing our canoe in a bright green canopy.

Cisco and I continued downstream. We handled the frequent rapids well. Usually they were characterized by a single chute with a fair drop, followed by a short pool. At the confluence of Bell Branch and Abrams Creek, we stopped to try some fishing. While getting out of the canoe I noticed a pile of crushed crayfish bones on a rock. It was otter scat. Though crayfish are the main fare for the otter, they also eat some fish and frogs. I would like to know some of their fishing secrets.

Otters are again inhabiting the park, as they did before white men set foot in the mountains. For half a century, the Smokies were without this playful and sociable water creature, as it had fallen victim to the logger and the trapper. In 1986, a group was released into Abrams Creek. The following year, I had the pleasure of seeing one frolicking in Abrams, near the Little Bottoms campsite. Several of the initial introduction groups began reproducing in the wild. More of the otters were introduced in the Little River watershed a year later. In January 1994, more than one hundred otters were released throughout the park, from Cosby Creek westward, in streams both large and small.

Dependent on external devices to catch my fish, I brought out my spinning reel and my rod, which was ready with a white spinner lure on the line. I began working my way along a large, shaded pool that lay upstream from the Bell Branch–Abrams Creek confluence. On my first cast I snagged the lure on an overhanging dogwood tree on the far bank. I waded into the creek to retrieve it, gasping at the tickling-cold water. I had to wade across up to my neck, while holding the rod high over my head out of the water, in order to retrieve the lure. On my way back, I watched Cisco lose purchase while casting, slipping off a rock and falling into the water up to his waist. We were both thankful for a warm day, as in colder weather we would have suffered miserably after our dunkings.

I continued fishing up the creek, and before long I had a fish hooked. It hit the spinner like a bolt of lightning as soon as the silver and white lure hit water. The fish turned its body perpendicular to the line and pulled with all its might. As I got him to the bank, my intuition was confirmed. It was a redeye, also known as a rock bass. These river dwellers are real fighters. Many an angler has been stunned when he has seen the relatively small size of such a fierce fish.

I quickly landed two more while making my way toward the next rapids upstream. I remembered the ranger at Abrams Creek telling us this was good bass water, as I released my fourth fish, a smallmouth, also plentiful in this stretch of Abrams Creek. When we returned to the canoe, Cisco announced that he had caught a few redeye and a sucker, an ugly, inedible forage fish with big lips that scours the creek bottom for food. It is a favorite of otters. We set our rods and ourselves back in the craft and paddled on.

Late that afternoon, we ran headlong into a sharp bend in the river. A large, long-dead oak had fallen across most of the river, channeling the fury of the water. The powerful current forced us to the outside of the bend, ramming the canoe into the tree and upsetting our balance. Always calm, Cisco pushed the canoe off the tree with his paddle; suddenly, just before tipping over, we sprang free.

We entered a wide shallow area that was choked with exposed boulders, through which we picked and pushed our way. Looking back, I could see Chilhowee Mountain beyond the river valley. After another sharp bend veering to the right, we passed through a series of fast drops into another large pool, and I thought I recognized this as our planned camping area, Shootly Branch. A look at the quad map confirmed this, and we pulled up at a small, shaded, gravel bar beside the gently gurgling creek.

Both Cisco and I were eager to fish after our earlier successes. So we unloaded our gear at a flat spot across Shootly Branch from the gravel bar, promising to set up camp later. I headed to the creek and immediately landed a jumping, fighting, foot-long rainbow trout. Cisco was still setting up his fly rod, an activity he expedited after seeing my fish. I excitedly headed downstream; my plan was to hike down streamside and then fish back up to the campsite. On the way, I slipped and nearly fractured my skull as I hurriedly crossed Abrams on the aptly described "slipperiest rocks in the Smokies."

Abrams Creek is unique among streams in the Smokies. It drains the area known as Cades Cove, a rustic former highlander community now maintained by the Park Service to illustrate the period when early settlers lived there. The cove's open pastures, surrounded on all sides by the mountains, support a herd of cattle and some horses, as well as deer and other wild creatures. The animal waste and the beasts' churning up mud on the creek's banks combine to create a silt unlike that found in other mountain creeks. This silt sticks to every rock between the cove and Chilhowee Lake. So the rocks in the creek are as slippery as ice. Fishing Abrams Creek is frankly dangerous, an agility test that no one passes.

Below the campsite, I clambered over downed trees, through tangled vines, and under overhanging limbs as I worked my way downstream along the bank. After a quarter-mile, I began fishing my way up a wide pool. Within fifteen minutes I had caught and released three redeyes. Such a fun fish to catch—they strike the lure with a vengeance and fight for their lives.

After a long cast, which I retrieved through a mild riffle, I hooked a trout—a nice ten-inch rainbow. I kept it on my improvised stringer: a cord tied to a belt loop on my shorts. The fish stayed in the water as I alternately slipped, fell, and waded my way upstream. It is hard to sneak up on the fish of Abrams Creek, but the canoe was taking us to waters little fished, so stealth mattered less than usual.

When the sun was long gone from the creek, I was ready to warm up and headed for camp. My wet feet felt like numb stumps, doing nothing for my agility in negotiating the slick rocks. Dusk approached as I arrived at the campsite pool. I positioned myself to work the deepest section of the pool, allowing my spinner to sink a bit lower than usual. As I slowly reeled in, I got a vicious strike. My rod bent nearly ninety degrees; its tip was twitching with life. A big one was on the line, and I slowly worked it in as I edged toward the bank. The fish was making its way downstream.

Suddenly my line broke, leaving me bitterly disappointed. After all, I had been fishing Abrams Creek for a few years, never quite landing a "Big Daddy" trout. Maybe the fish I had just lost was the monster I had been seeking. Although I had caught many fish that day, including four trout, at camp all I could talk about was the one that got away.

Soon we had a heap of wood piled up for the fire. While the temperature was a pleasant sixty-five degrees, we needed extra wood so that we could get red-hot coals ready for cooking the steaks for steak sandwiches. Two Coleman lanterns hanging on an old holly tree cast light, while the murmur of the creek helped give the campsite a tranquil feeling. We settled back into the comfort of our camp chairs and discussed the day's events.

"Why did I buy that two-pound test line?" I moaned repeatedly, still grieving over the anonymous fish. This was the first time I had strayed from my usual four-pound line, which I deemed best for angling in the Smokies. Earlier, in our haste while buying supplies, Cisco had recommended that I get the two-pound test line instead of the four-pound. "Have you ever caught a trout over two pounds in the Smokies?" he asked. I admitted I had not and went ahead with the purchase. What we had failed to take into account, however, was the tenacious nature of these mountain fish. Their strenuous resistance to being reeled in must have put extra strain on the puny two-pound line. I suppose that I blamed Cisco for my lost fish, and I vowed to stick with my intuition the next time I bought line. Before this trip ended, though, as the canoe took us downriver, there would be many more fish to battle.

By now the coals were glowing. I placed a light, metal grill over the fire ring rock and laid our steaks on top of the grill. Soon we dined on the succulent steak sandwiches, along with Cole slaw and barbecue beans. As we ate, a flash of light brightened the western sky through the trees. As we continued looking that way, the flashes became more frequent, signaling the impending arrival of a thunderstorm. After supper we retired under the tarp. Soon the thunder, lightning, and rain came, splattering the new leaves and lulling us to sleep. That night I dreamed of the trout that got away.

In 1957, in an environmental near-disaster orchestrated by governmental biologists, all the fish got away. To "improve" trout fishing in Abrams Creek and the river into which it flowed, the Little Tennessee, the scientists poisoned the two waterways with a chemical called *rotenone*, to kill all the fish. The Little Tennessee was scheduled to be dammed, after which the biologists would restock the waters with trout, making them particularly rich for trout fishing. That was the theory. After this ill-conceived scheme was carried out, various dead fish were collected from Abrams Creek and analyzed. One fish, dubbed the Smoky madtom, was found to be unique to these waters. The government biologists, at a single blow, had both discovered and extirpated a species of fish.

But the story does not end there. On the other side of the Little Tennessee flows Citico Creek, which is in the Cherokee National Forest. A population of madtoms was found there in 1980. Government biologists once again got busy, this time amending their horrible error. Madtoms have been reintroduced into Abrams, and they are thought to be reproducing, though not at the rate they once did. While fishing this remote area of the creek in the summer of 1993, I ran into some madtom hunters, who were having trouble finding the rare fish. I cannot help wondering what other environmentally unsound projects are being carried out today.

The sun was already shining when I woke the next day, at 7:30. The crispness of the air made me thirst for piping hot coffee. I lit my stove and soon indulged my desire, burning my mouth in my haste to fish. Leaving the sleeping Cisco to his own devices, I picked up my rod and headed to the nearby pool. Casting into the deepest section of the pool, I drew a strike right away.

Visions of rainbow trout danced in my head as my early morning caffeine buzz was augmented with an adrenaline rush. I had adjusted the drag on my reel and now was ready for hard-fighting monster trout. Lo and behold, the line snapped again. The fish was gone. I was crushed. I dejectedly returned to camp, there to muster the courage I needed to continue fishing in the face of such humiliating failure.

Cisco was up and tending a fire. We toasted bagels, which we then smothered in cream cheese and washed down with General Foods' Cafe Français. The simple repast revitalized me, so I went about breaking down camp as Cisco got a few casts in at the pool. At 10 A.M. we shoved off, now under a darkening, cloudy sky. Our violation of one important rule of canoe camping was about to haunt us.

Little did we know at the time what a good camping site we had found. We had made it safely to camp with all our gear still dry, a fact that allowed us to enjoy the previous night. But the river was about to turn on us. Starting shortly below Shootly Branch, the river changed character. Numerous sharp bends, narrow river width, churning splashy water, and frequent deep drops slowly unnerved us. We made our way through many rapids, but our canoe steadily was filling with water that splashed in while we negotiated the rapids. We had had a low clearance to begin with, from all the equipment we had packed. We wanted to bail, but the swift flow of the creek would not allow that. As soon as we regrouped from one drop, we had to negotiate another. Occasionally I would force a stop and bail, but then I was so nervous that I wanted to keep going, to get the difficult rapids behind us. Having never been down the creek, I did not know how far downstream we would have to travel to do that.

As Cisco and I tried to traverse the creek from the right side to the left in order to reach a gentler chute, we rammed a rock. The canoe listed, and water rushed in from its upstream side. As the craft quickly filled with water, I dislodged us with a mighty push of my paddle, just before we went over a four-foot drop. In the midst of the struggle, our small yellow dry bag, holding our wallets and keys, fell overboard, shooting down the rapids and out of sight. Had I followed a cardinal rule of canoeing and secured my gear in the boat, we still would have had our necessities with us. Instant retrieval was impossible, so we unloaded the canoe, dumped the water, and proceeded on, hoping to catch up with our valuables.

By now we were frazzled, and our confidence was bruised.

At an acute bend to the right, the main thrust of water made a foamy five-foot drop, tightly surrounded by two large boulders, and rushed onward down a narrow rock-lined ravine. Cisco announced that, if he had anything to do with it, we were not going down that way. So, with some fancy twisting and turning, we made it down the shallower left side. Our haste to catch up with the floating yellow bag made us braver and more decisive than we otherwise could have been.

The river widened immediately above Chilhowee Lake, in an area I recognized from previous fishing trips. We felt sure we could find our dry bag just below the final rapids, near the mouth of the lake. Soon we floated on the lake, searching in vain for our little yellow bag. We paddled down the long, flooded river valley and before long came upon a fisherman. No, he had not seen the bag. We were cold, tired, and hungry; we had a mess on our hands. We quickly ate some fruit and other leftovers and then paddled back to the river's mouth. We had to recover the bag somehow, so we set about looking back up the creek.

Cisco left, going upstream while I stayed near the gear. Some suspicious-looking anglers idled nearby, and I did not want to leave our equipment to their mercy. Having already lost our identification and car keys, I guess I was unusually wary of my fellow outdoorsmen. I made the most of my time by pulling out my rod and casting. Subsequently I snagged a twelve-inch trout. I put him on the melting ice and moved upstream a bit. I cast the lure toward the head of a pool and thought I was hung when I felt a heavy resistance on the end. But then my line shot out toward the far bank. I had a lunker hooked, and he was running for his life. I slowly worked the fish toward me. He was so close, a large colorful rainbow. I reached to grasp him but he exploded, dashing off again. My line screamed off the reel. I tightened my grip on the rod, keeping a precarious hold on my pole. Then all of the sudden—pop! The line had broken again!

Hands shaking, I hurriedly put on another lure and cast. Boom! I got another strike right away. I worked the fish near me. I pulled him out of the water, to flip him onto the bank, desperately wishing I had a net. As I got him out of the water, he twitched, and again the blasted line snapped! I was beyond shock. My head swam. My heart pounded. My eyes watered. I stumbled in disbelief at my bad luck as I thrashed my way back to the canoe.

Since the suspicious fishermen had left the area, I decided to forge upstream and help Cisco with the recovery effort. Maybe I could forget about trout fishing for a while. I alternated between slipping over the rocks, crawling through rhododendron, and dodging small trees on the junglelike creek bank. No sign of Cisco or the bag. After an interminable period of such rummaging, I spotted Cisco. He was about to cross the creek, and when he saw me, he yelled, "I've spotted the bag. It's on your side, behind those rocks."

I saw it. The bag lay in an eddy surrounded on three sides by boulders. We were lucky to have seen it. The water was deep, and I was almost totally immersed when I reached the bag. I was shivering by the time I reached the bank, bag in hand. Moving quickly to keep warm, we returned to the canoe as rapidly as we could, but it took us at least an hour of fighting along the river's edge before we reached the boat. We were exhausted but felt relieved at having our keys. Cisco and I had a two-mile paddle ahead of us across the mercifully placid lake.

By the time we arrived at my Jeep, loaded our gear, got to Cisco's truck, and headed home, darkness was falling. Driving home, I recalled the excitement of canoe camping in the Smokies: the craggy rapids of Abrams Creek, the slippery rocks and chilly waters, the feisty bass and trout. I had every reason for satisfaction and none for complaint. All the same, the next time I would bring that four-pound test line.

Backwoods Anglers Vie for Smoky Mountain Rainbow

Off-trail Hiking and Fishing on the Smokies' Western Edge

May is an exciting time to be in the Great Smoky Mountains National Park. The once-dormant forest springs into life. Green, growing leaves return to the trees; colorful wildflowers carpet the woodland floor. Black bears, many now with cubs, emerge from hibernation. Myriad insects crawl, hop, and fly. The cycle begins anew. As the weather becomes milder and the streams warm up to merely bone-chilling cold, the fish begin to feed. For the trout angler, the winter wait is over. Lures and flies have been assembled, instructional books reread again. It is now time for action.

Over seven hundred miles of fishable streams flow through the Smokies. Roads parallel many of these streams, affording easy access. But this accessibility has drawbacks. Too many anglers in a stream make the trout even more skittish and cautious than usual. And the sight and sound of cars droning nearby negates an important aspect of the mountain experience—the sense of getting away from it all. I find it irritating, too, when windshield tourists stop and watch me fish. I feel under pressure to catch one for them, which almost never happens. And when one car stops, other cars pull over to see what the first car stopped to see, and before long you are fishing for an audience.

Backcountry trails lead to and parallel other streams, eliminating the auto tourist audience and the many fishermen who are not willing to hike for a head-to-head battle with the wary trout. And, finally, some streams flow through trackless wilderness where the fisherman must negotiate unknown terrain as well as the elusive quarry.

Bearing all this in mind and propelled by a serious case of fishing fever, my adventurous hiking buddy John Cox and I opted for the two-pronged challenge of off-trail hiking and trout fishing in the Panther Creek and Abrams Creek areas on the Smokies' western edge.

John and I had our gear loaded into our packs as we sped south from Knoxville on Highway 129 near Chilhowee Lake. This body of water, artificially created in 1959, is one of the chain of lakes that often is called the Finger Lakes of the Smokies. Born of the Little Tennessee River, a premier trout stream in its own right before it was dammed, Chilhowee and its companion lakes, Cheoah and Calderwood, form part of the southern and western borders of the national park. Chilhowee is home to bream, bass, and trout. The mountains rise directly out of the lake, making Highway 129 a very scenic roadway. But the beautiful setting has become a veritable magnet for dubious characters. I can only speculate that roadside camping allows for easier beer runs. Such gatherings can spur theft and vandalism.

I was hesitant to leave my Jeep parked among such rabble. Instead I entrusted it to Charlie Lunsford, postmaster of the Tallassee community and owner of the Tallassee General Store along 129, a short way below the Chilhowee Dam. Bearded and tattooed, the Tallassee native does not look like my stereotype of a postmaster. But he is as friendly as can be, as is shown by the continual gatherings of amiable folks who congregate around his store, which sells everything from camping gear to old-fashioned dry goods. Charlie is, in effect, a catalog of information about the people and history of the locale. He offered to keep my Jeep behind his house, where it would be safe. I readily accepted his offer.

It was already six o'clock when Charlie dropped us off at a spot on the park border by the lake; I knew the place from previous forays and map examinations. It was the beginning of a route to Panther Creek. We promptly began a steep climb along a noisy little rivulet. The ground beneath my feet gave way, as I slid part of the way back down the sloping hill. At some points I grabbed at any vegetation I could use to pull me back up. As our path leveled off, we came to the first evidence of man's pre-park occupancy.

A set of ancient, rusty bedsprings and a collapsed shack were all the remains that the forces of nature had left of a past dwelling. We pressed on, veering left up a small hollow that evidently was recovering from a fairly recent fire. The trunks of still-living trees were blackened around their bases, and a tangle of briars reached out to scratch and snag skin, shirts, and packs. Beyond the brule, or burned-over area, we traversed a tiny gap that was our gateway into the Panther Creek watershed.

On our descent, we came across another old homesite, more obvious than the first. A crumbling chimney formed the centerpiece of a clearing that was being reclaimed by the encroaching forest. As at most old homesites, a small spring trickled nearby; this one, however, was surrounded by a muddy wallow, indicating the presence of wild boars. The clearing quickly disappeared as we followed a stream from the spring down a narrow hemlock-choked hollow. Soon the rushing sounds of Panther Creek announced our arrival at the old railroad grade alongside the stream. It was nearly seven o'clock as we fought our way through the neon-green spring forest along the faint, overgrown fisherman's trail.

As the creek twisted sharply northward, Panther Creek cascaded thirty feet over a bare rock face into a large pool. The spot, bare of vegetation, allowed more light than the surrounding dark forest; the effect was numinous, as if God had spotlighted it from heaven. Gray, pocked, water-worn boulders and the crashing white water stood out in bold relief under a gaping sky, framed by dense woods.

Darkness was imminent; we had to keep moving beyond this first of many awe-inspiring sights and sounds of the area. In twenty minutes we made our second wet crossing of the creek, to yet another former homesite that I had explored before. A ruined chimney stands there, too, among slim young pines. This spot is very flat, inside a bend of the creek, and heavily wooded, making it an ideal out-of-the-way fishing camp.

We immediately began setting up camp. By sundown we

had set up a friendly fire and a sturdy tarp, our defense against any possible spring thunderstorm. I then shaped some ground beef patties, as John set up a small, portable grill over the coals. Under the glow of the lantern, we dined on juicy cheeseburgers and potato salad. Even in mild temperatures, fresh meat can be a safe and tasty treat while camping. Freeze it at home and wrap it in foil, and it will be thawed by the time you arrive at the first campsite. This was our only big meal of the trip, since we were hiking off-trail. Pack weight becomes a particularly important consideration when fighting through dense woods and across steep terrain. For the rest of our trip, our supper entree was to be what we could obtain with rod and reel.

After our evening repast, we reclined by the fire on our closed-cell foam sleeping pads. For backpacking, I recommend these over air mattresses, which, in my estimation, are a failure waiting to happen. The last place I want an inflatable mattress is the woods, where sharp rocks and sticks abound. These mattresses can be used only when spread out for lying down on a tent floor. A rolled-up foam pad, in contrast, can be placed on a rock to function as a cushion during a rest; it can be folded in half by a fire, and a spark or stick will not damage it irreparably. Furthermore, an air mattress costs at least three times as much as a foam pad. An air mattress failure in mid-trip can make sleeping more difficult, turning a challenging backpacking excursion into a tiresome chore.

Discussing our fishing strategies for the next day, John and I promised to rise early, as Panther Creek babbled just over yonder. We retired under the tarp around eleven. Sometime in the night a rain fell, apparently steadily but not too hard, because the creek did not show any rise or murkiness the next morning. I awakened long enough to notice the precipitation but quickly fell asleep again, as no sleeping potion ever invented is as effective as raindrops drumming on a stretched tarp in the deep, dark woods.

The rain had stopped, leaving in its wake a cloudy sunrise that seduced me into remaining in my bag, half-asleep. I thought I was dreaming when I heard several dogs barking lustily, heading our way. I jumped out of my bag partially clothed and peered sleepy-eyed across the creek toward the ruckus. Suddenly, across the water a large animal shot out of the woods and into the creek, splashing its way directly toward me. I stood frozen in fear and disbelief as the tusky boar saw me and stopped in midstream. For a brief but seemingly endless moment, we were locked in a staring contest, his bloodshot eyes exuding fear and hate all at once.

Just as I nearly fainted from fright, the boar turned away and sped off into the woods, having decided to test fate against the dogs, who surely were accompanied by a hunter. The barking faded off in the distance and no gunshot sounded, so I assume that the boar escaped. Finding oneself face to face with such an animal in the wild is a rare experience. Usually, when a human spots wildlife, the animal almost invariably is running away and only the tail end is visible. That is good for the animal, for an animal that retains a healthy fear of man is the one that lives longest. Wild animals exist as part of the overall biological system of an area, not as a sideshow for humans to gawk at.

All hunting is illegal within the park. It is disheartening that lawbreakers cannot appreciate the value of the national park and all the flora and fauna within its boundaries, rather than defiling it. Plenty of hunting areas abound near the Smokies, so there is no need to hunt in the park. But the boar is an exotic animal, and the Park Service is attempting to eradicate or at least control the population of these destructive creatures. Boars root up the ground, destroying acres of wildflowers and other plants, encouraging erosion. And they eat food that could have supported nondestructive animals indigenous to the park. Moreover, to study the effects of the boars on the land they roam and compare it with areas where no boars exist, the Park Service has erected at least two boar exclosures around areas that are kept boar-free.

Both John and I were fully awake after the startling, almost surreal incident. John made a monster batch of buckwheat pancakes, drenched in syrup and butter, which we washed down with rich, nearly scalding coffee. As we ate, John wondered aloud, "Did the hunter see us? And if he did, was he mad at us?" I replied, "He may have been fearful we would report him to park authorities." If caught, the violator faces a maximum fine of ten thousand dollars, up to two years in jail, and confiscation of all items used in committing the offense, including any vehicle.

Full and satisfied, I left camp with rod in hand, moving upstream to fish. John hiked down to the point where the stream empties into Chilhowee Lake, intending to fish his way back to the campsite. As I began casting, the clouds broke, and the day turned partly sunny. While I fished upstream, a chill crept over me. The absence of trails in the densely forested banks forced me to travel through the cold water. Unfortunately my luck was less satisfying than the splendor of the spring scenery. The trees and other plants looked so vibrant that it seemed I could see them greening and growing before my eyes. "It's a great day to be alive," I thought as I rounded a bend in the stream to find an abandoned flatbed rail car, which seemed badly out of place now in these thick woods. I could barely squeeze my body through the flourishing greenery. Though I tried several different lures, several hours and many casts later I had netted just two puny rainbows. I trudged dejectedly back to camp.

John loitered about our campsite, announcing that he had been shut out. It was five in the evening already, and we had meager supplies for dinner. I decided to head downriver and try my hand on the lower reaches of Panther Creek, where I had been lucky before. Within five minutes I hooked the largest rainbow I had ever pulled out of that creek. It was easily a foot long and had been fished out of a tiny pool not much bigger than the fish itself. Trout are hard to figure out, because they feed with maddening irregularity. This adds to the challenge of fishing for them but can tax the angler's sanity. On this occasion, the fishing gods were on my side, and in short order I had nabbed three more healthy trout. By six o'clock, I was prancing back to camp proudly toting our evening fare.

Dusk came as we feasted on sautéed trout and baked beans. The lantern brightened our corner of the woods as we whiled away the hours discussing the pitfalls and joys of trout fishing in the Smokies. We awoke at dawn, this day to the sound of chirping birds rather than to a splashing boar, having slept in

FISHING PANTHER CREEK IN SPRING. While I fished upstream, a chill crept over me. The dense forest on the banks forced me to travel through the cold water.

the open, cool air; we were glad that no rain had fallen. As usual, a night under the stars left me feeling especially invigorated, ready for a big day in the mountains. It was fifty-eight degrees, and we determined to get a quick start before the day warmed up. Our task, using a map and compass, was to hike through hilly woods with no trails from Panther Creek to a remote stretch of Abrams Creek.

To facilitate an early start, we had prepared our packs the night before. All equipment we lashed on and battened down, to assure its arrival at our destination. In off-trail hiking, rhododendron arms, tree and shrub limbs, and thrashing through the woods generally can take its toll on gear and clothing. Button everything you wear while off-trail. Excessively loose clothing can get snagged. Long pants and long-sleeved shirts reduce the chances of getting abrasions. Protruding limbs and sticks offer an underestimated danger of scratching or poking you in the eye, out where rescue is difficult or impossible. An off-trail hiker must exercise utmost caution traveling in trackless wilderness.

CLIMBING A SHALE RIDGE. At the confluence of Murray Branch and Panther Creek, half an hour from the campsite, we tacked westward, scaling a slippery shale ridge.

Carrying the United States quadrangle map and a reliable Suunto compass tied to my belt loop with a strong cord, I marched north with John beside Panther Creek. At the confluence of Murray Branch and Panther Creek, half an hour up from the campsite, we tacked westward, scaling a slippery shale ridge. About a hundred feet up, I saw three thick, rusty steel cables extending downward from the ridge. They may have been relics left over from the railroad logging days. Or they may have been used to extract the shale upon which we stood. After testing one for strength, John and I used it as a climbing "rope" most of the way up the ridge, until I came to the place where it was spiked down to a large embedded rock.

Near the top of the ridge, an open area of loose shale afforded a picturesque view of the lower Panther Creek Valley. Parson Bald rose in the background, framed by a stand of tall pines. The rugged splendor reminded me of how well a forest can recover from such human depredations as logging and mining.

Once atop the low ridge (elevation 1,400 feet), I hoped to find an old road, appearing on a 1931 map of the Smokies, that leads to Shootly Branch, which we would follow to Abrams Creek. But time and the elements had obliterated the old path. With no physical signs to follow, we checked the compass and headed north. As I compared our location with where I thought we were on the map, I often felt I knew just where we were. I was wrong.

To get to Abrams Creek, we had to cross Huckleberry Branch. The next major creek was Shootly Branch, our goal. Along the way, we crossed a small streamlet that I supposed was Huckleberry Branch. So the second creek we crossed we followed, down to Abrams Creek. As it turned out, we had followed Huckleberry Branch, not Shootly Branch. We were one and a half rough, overgrown miles from our intended destination. John and I trudged back up Huckleberry Branch, passing an open former homesite where the narrow valley widened and then closed back up—an isolated site, by any measure. We resumed our northward course toward the Shootly Branch watershed. An off-trail axiom: You have never traveled as far as your exhaustion leads you to believe.

As we continued over the piney hills, John suddenly yelled. He was standing before a rattlesnake, which emitted its customary warning rattle from a shallow hollow. The viper defiantly held its ground. We wisely passed around it, maintaining a northwesterly course. There are two dangerous snakes in the Smokies: the rattler and the copperhead. Most encounters occur when a hiker comes upon a snake that is sunning itself on a rock—often near a stream, in the case of the copperhead. But the snakes usually do not want trouble and rarely strike unless stepped on or similarly disturbed. I consider it a privilege to see these cold-blooded creatures in their natural habitat. Unfortunately, some people feel compelled to kill every snake they see. Don't make that mistake. We need snakes, because they are part of nature's equation.

We ranged over small knobs (rocky hillocks), their tops so crowded with young pines that we had to walk sideways among them, knocking dead branches from their lower trunks. Each branch released a fragrant spray of pine dust as it fell to the ground. Down we slid through steep-sided, rocky, rhododendron-snarled ravines. After going up and down in this way for awhile, John and I finally took our chances, tracking a meandering rill and hoping that it was part of the Shootly Branch watershed. It was. Our spirits soared as we followed the ever-widening small creek down to its confluence with Abrams Creek, location of our planned campsite. It was 11:30 A.M., and we had been on the move for three and a half hours.

As we stalked off-trail through dense, trackless timberland, all sorts of debris from trees and bushes had settled in our hair, on our necks, and in our clothes. Wood sap and other gunk had left us sweaty and dirty. But this was clean and natural dirt, unlike the grime from a meatpacking plant or an auto garage. Rather, this dirt recalled the innocent grit of a childhood sandlot football game.

I shed my clothes and jumped into refreshing Abrams Creek, enjoying the respite from my filthy state. I scrubbed and frolicked briefly in the icy water. At sixty-eight degrees, the day was still fairly cool as I lit my stove and brewed some coffee to get pepped up for a day of trout fishing in America.

John hurriedly grabbed his rod and disappeared downstream. I perused my lures, choosing a single-hook orange Roostertail, and tied it on my line. Official park regulations require the use of single-hook artificial lures only. I pressed up Abrams Creek, which flowed swift, cold, and clear. I positioned myself at the base of a large pool upstream, below a drop where the creek constricted, flanked on the left by a large boulder. I cast my lure into a riffle at the head of the deep pool and let it sink to a count of five, then retrieved it slowly. I had no takers. I cast again.

Suddenly my line ran counter to the current. Adrenaline pulsed through my veins, as I set the hook and landed a defiant rainbow. I unhooked him and shakily ran a cord through his lower lip, then tied the cord onto the belt loop of my shorts. Continuing to work the pool, I landed another trout and two redeye or rock bass, releasing the bass.

I stumbled onward upstream, through a shallow, rocky area

with few promising holes. Nonetheless I fished the area hard, with no luck. Then I struggled upstream through the creek. By the time I reached Bell Branch a mile upstream, I was dog tired and chilled to the marrow of my bones. A mile of travel along a rocky, vegetation-choked mountain stream will wear down even the hardiest fisherman. The sun was long gone. The stringer of five rainbows and the memory of the other trout and redeye I had caught and then released was gratifying, but the difficult return journey to the campsite was uppermost in my mind.

A faint fisherman's trail shadows the creek, but it still took well over an hour to return. My struggle led through rhododendron thickets, over fallen trees, and amid poking branches; the fact that I had a fishing rod in one hand and a stringer of trout in the other made the hike more difficult. Finally I spotted the flickering firelight across the stream, indicating the campsite. After fording Abrams Creek in total darkness, I saw John tending the welcoming fire.

John recounted a taxing day. The riverside downstream had been profoundly overgrown and the rocks especially slippery, making for some difficult fishing. So he had returned fairly early, spending the day reading and exploring the locale. He found and followed an old road—another remnant of man in the mountains—along the north side of Shootly Branch until it petered out. We both were weary yet anxious for a toothsome meal.

I savored a cup of coffee, while John sliced onions and potatoes for hash browns. I cleaned the trout and dipped them in a plastic freezer bag full of cornmeal. Soon the aroma of frying fresh trout permeated our camp as I put away the resealable bag of meal for future use. Shortly we dined on tasty breaded trout, steamy hash browns, strong hot coffee, and cool mountain water. Neither John nor I said, "It doesn't get any better than this." That went without saying. After cleaning up after ourselves, we spread out our bedrolls and were lulled to sleep by the white noise of rushing Abrams Creek.

Following a sound night's slumber, I felt refreshed but flushed all over. I had fishing fever. The previous two days of angling had only fueled my desire to read the flowing waters and place

an enticing lure before a hungry trout. The first big pool upstream from our bivouac produced one trout and a couple of
redeye. I then pressed directly upriver to Bell Branch, to the
point where I had fished the day before. The sun bore down on
my shirtless back, as I made my way up the alternating sections
of rapids and slack water. As the heat flared, so did the clouds.
Standing in the chilled waters, I reeled in and then released a
few redeye.

I moved on toward a curious old structure on the east bank
that stood about twelve feet high. The rectangular flat-topped
pyramid measured about ten feet by five feet, and was constructed
of native stones. At first it seemed to be an old railroad trestle,
part of an old mill, or the remnant of a road bridge. But the
1931 map of the Smokies shows a bridge crossing Abrams Creek
and leading to some houses up a small rill on the east bank.
Whatever the structure was, it had to have withstood at least
fifty years of the periodic and not at all uncommon flooding of
the mountain-draining watershed.

Nearby I found an inviting pool. Although thunder rumbled
in the distance, the sun shone overhead, so I waded into the
water, a little nervous about the possibility of lightning. I cast
into the head of the pool and reeled in a colorful rainbow. On
the next cast, I caught his brother. Rainbow trout are not native to Smoky Mountain waters. The only native trout is the
brook trout, which technically is not a trout at all, but a char
from Arctic waters, forced south by the last Ice Age. During the
logging days at the beginning of this century, streams became
warm, silted, and unfit for the finicky brook trout. Some early
naturalists noticed the absence of the char and so restocked virtually every stream in the park with rainbows, native to the West,
and later with brown trout that were brought from Germany
and Scotland. These fish were brought into the mountain streams
by rail, mule, and foot, and through the years they expanded
their range. Now the rainbow is king in the Smokies, and the
native brook has been pushed back into remote headwater streams
high in the mountains, living mostly in creeks where fishing is
barred. The Park Service avidly keeps an eye on the "brookie,"
protecting and preserving its domain.

In my excitement, I discounted the threat of rain, figuring that I could fish through the impending thunderstorm and return to a drying camp. The fever had gone to my brain, because the last place you should be when it is thundering is in a creek. In case of a storm, I usually find refuge, preferably within a rhododendron thicket or under a small or medium-sized tree; a large tree is more likely to draw lightning. But this time I fished on until my reel began seizing as a result of too many unexpected dunkings in Abrams Creek and elsewhere. Now I carry a small vial of machine oil to grease a seizing reel.

When fishing along the slick bottom of Abrams, you are going to slip and fall. The trick is to keep your reel out of the water when falling. But your safety should take precedence over the safety of your reel, so be sure of every step you take, whether it is on trail, off the trail, or in flowing water.

I worked my way back to camp, fiddling with the reel and getting it to work well enough to harvest two more trout. The rain never fell on my section of the woods. Back at our camp, John had a fire going and was using a deft hand to filet some fat redeye he had caught. He then began working on my rainbow. I made Cajun rice. For the third night running, we dined on fish caught by our own capable hands. I felt manly and self-reliant.

As the sun set on the vivid green forest, we relaxed by the fire, listening to the resonant sounds of Shootly Branch. I hummed Hank Williams's tune "Ramblin' Man." We reflected on our four days; I mourned their end. I stayed awake until late, reading by lantern light the Steinbeck novel *The Grapes of Wrath*. Slowly I fell into the dreamless sleep attendant upon a hard but satisfying day.

We awoke around 8:30 A.M. to a cloudy sky, ate a morning meal, and then packed up and headed into the woods. Our packs were much lighter than when we had entered the forest. John and I forded Abrams Creek for the last time, as a light drizzle began falling. After changing from our water-wear tennis shoes into our hiking boots, we sauntered up a small rivulet across and just downstream from Shootly Branch. The leaves of the woods in the tiny valley were colored countless shades of green.

Our route led to an old pine needle–carpeted road. As we walked up the road through Happy Valley Gap, an almost continuous line of blooming mountain laurel bade us farewell, in this trip's final display of the Smokies' beauty.

Beyond the gap we headed downhill and out of the park to Happy Valley Road. A friendly local fellow came along and gave us a lift in the bed of his ancient Ford pickup, carrying us back to my Jeep. That short, quiet ride in the old truck bed, with the wind blowing about us and tranquil Happy Valley slipping past, carried us back to the "outside" world, beyond the forests and mountains.

Now, however, we were different. We knew that we could journey in the wilderness, using just a map, a compass, and our wits. As outdoor authority Leroy G. Fox put it: "Deep inside you know you have achieved a rare freedom to roam where you will in rugged mountains, perhaps even to step where no man has stepped before."

In the Valley of the Ford

Fontana Dam to Cades Cove

We crossed Fontana Dam by auto. A steady shower obscured views of the lake and mountains. The windshield wipers beat time like a metronome. Rain again. Experienced backpackers learn to prepare for and live with rain, if they spend time in the temperate rain forest known as the Great Smoky Mountains. It rains more than ninety inches a year at the highest elevations, the precipitation declining with altitude.

My partner John Cox and I set out on this particular adventure at nineteen hundred feet, where the AT leaves the national park to cross Fontana Dam on its way to Springer Mountain in Georgia. We geared up quickly, strapping on our packs and marching north up the AT into the rain. March was ending, and the high mountains still were cloaked in their drab winter garb. Spring had come to the calendar, but we wanted to see evidence of the year's rebirth in the Smokies.

The muddy trail to Shuckstack Mountain was shrouded in an ever-thickening fog. In the soaked hardwood forest, visibility was down to about twenty feet. Stark, barren oak and poplar branches drifted in and out of view like ghost trees along a stairwell to hell. We huffed and puffed during the steep two-mile climb to the top of Little Shuckstack. Three and a half miles beyond the trailhead, we reached the small side trail leading a tenth of a mile to the Shuckstack fire tower. Due to the fog, we decided against the tower climb.

After a short descent, we were in Sassafras Gap (elevation

3,650 feet) and at a trail junction. To take a break in the rain would have been pointless, though the rain seemed to be tapering off. John and I turned east down the Lost Cove Trail. The slender, steep path dropped off the mountainside in a series of switchbacks. Wet leaves covered the little-used trail, making it treacherous. As if on cue, my boots slipped out from under me on one of the switchbacks. The weight of a full pack brought me down with a splash. The squishy landing on the disintegrating leaves muddied my legs and buttocks.

I got up, grimy but none the worse for it. John stood above me, laughing. But in that stretch three-quarters of a mile long, he was to go down, too. Finally we came to Lost Cove Creek, with its gentler grade down the tight, gloomy gulf. John and I left the fog on the ridgetop, along with its wind-sculpted trees in tortured shapes, and followed the swollen, roiling torrent a mile to our campsite, Upper Lost Cove (elevation 2,040 feet). It is a small, lightly used, out-of-the-way campsite, lying on a fair slope.

Our first order of business was to string up a tarp, which we slung low with the help of rope and a tree. The rain ceased, but we could not count on it to stop for long. In our darkened, cloud-covered valley, I fetched water from the creek. During fall and winter, especially after a rain, creek water often contains bits of leaves and sediment of every description. So I have made a practice not to scrutinize for clarity every cup I drink, at least not as long as I am far from civilization.

Water in the Smokies generally runs cold and clear. In my opinion, it is fit for consumption, but the Park Service recommends boiling or treating the bountiful liquid. Personally, I don't bother. I have always gulped my fill mouth-to-stream and never had any problem. But neither have I had giardia, a harmful organism that causes severe intestinal disorders. Either I have an iron gut, or my system is used to the water. As far as I know, few have been sickened by these mountain waters. That is not to say that it is not possible. One stream, Abrams Creek, flows through the animal pastureland of Cades Cove, rendering it undrinkable. Of course, in my early days of backpacking in the Smokies, I drank it right down. Now I would not drink it, but that is the only exception. And unless I find myself retching, I will continue to drink this, the finest water I have ever consumed. Mountaineers displaced after the park's establishment missed their homeland springs terribly. I can see why.

John started a fire while I brewed coffee and changed into clean clothes. I saw no pre-park homesites as I scoured the heavily timbered forest for firewood. Many backcountry campsites were former homes of early settlers. During spring, these homesites are easily identified by the perennial flowering plants that the homesteaders planted in their yards. It is quite a startling sight to see a straight row of jonquils line a road that has become a trail. As night fell, I shucked and foil-wrapped four ears of corn for roasting in the fire. As usual, our first night's fare featured heavy perishables to cook over hot coals. Tonight we would have grilled steak sandwiches topped with sautéed onions.

John and I stuffed ourselves and lounged about the fire, digesting our food in the unusually warm air. We turned in early and opted for the roofed shelter, in case the rain decided to take an encore. The night was dry, and the next morning dawned cloudy and cool. The valley was still damp as John roused a morning fire. His thick slabs of crackling bacon dripped grease onto the hot coals, while I scrambled eggs on my stove. We quaffed hot coffee and cleaned up quickly after breakfast, eager to reach Eagle Creek.

But first John and I had a hike of one and a half miles on Lost Cove Creek. Not far below the campsite, we came to our first ford. The small creek crashed and roared, running high due to rain. The exposed rocks lay slick and wet. Yet we both made it across dry; then again, and again, and again. All the while, the temporarily dingy creek widened, making each successive crossing increasingly difficult.

Ten or more crossings later, we came to the confluence with Eagle Creek. John had had a foot dunking, but at least, after that, he could slosh right across a stream. With a little luck, I made it through unscathed. We stopped where Lost Cove Creek and Eagle Creek merge, and John changed into dry socks.

Nearby is the site of the popular Lost Cove backcountry campsite. The clouds were breaking; the morning was warm-

FORDING LOWER EAGLE CREEK. Rock-hopping was not an option on this first of many wet fords.

ing swiftly. I stripped to a T-shirt and shorts, then we sallied forth up the Eagle Creek Trail in an open area that would be covered by Fontana Lake if it were at full pool; but, as usual, it wasn't. I have seen it at full pool only once, and then, ironically, it was flooded and a few feet above pool.

We hiked up the wide creekside trail, tracing Horseshoe Bend among the white pines and passing the Pinnacle Creek Trail intersection a mile above the lake. The two of us continued on the west side of the creek, where the sun was drying the forest floor, contributing a woodsy aroma to the fresh, post-shower air. We came to our first ford of Eagle Creek. Rock-hopping was not an option on this first of many wet fords. Eagle simply is too wide and deep at this point.

After securely tying my boots onto my pack, I put on my Converse Chuck Taylor fording sneakers. Then I waded into the bone-chilling water, following John's lead. I was thigh deep at the deepest point of the creek, so it was heartening to see that the sun had come out for good that day. Our hike alternated between making more numbing fords and walking beneath tunnel-like rhododendron thickets.

Later we arrived at a top-notch campsite, Lower Ekaneetlee. Located at the confluence of Ekaneetlee Creek and Eagle Creek, it is a flat area carpeted with, and partly shaded by, fragrant pine. The time was eleven o'clock, and we were quite excited at the prospect of fishing for trout for the first time that year. I hastily readied my poles and retrieved my lures from their usual pocket of my external frame pack.

Surprisingly, these frames are losing in popularity; I believe them to be the overall best choice for backpackers, though internals are best for off-trail backpacking. Externals are much more economical. Organizationally, too, they are superior; you easily can arrange and access your gear in the many pockets they have. What most novices do not realize is that the pack functions as a sort of campsite chest of drawers. Your pack spends much more time propped against a tree than it does bouncing along on your back. Moreover, an external is cooler. An internal sits directly on your back, preventing heat from escaping and creating a sweaty spot in even the coldest weather. An external has a mesh band on your back, with an air pocket between you and the pack frame, allowing heat to escape.

John dashed up the trail to try his luck upstream, while I rushed down to waters that I had secretly scouted on the hike up. The fishing rodeo was on.

"A glorious day to be trout fishing in the Smokies," I thought to myself as I stepped into the chilly water under a bold blue sky and made my first cast. "Why aren't the fish biting?" I asked myself two hours later. I climbed onto a sunny rock to see if my numbed feet were still attached to my legs. I could not have asked for more beautiful scenery: clear creek, tumbling falls, mountain flora. But I wanted a multi-hued rainbow trout! I decided to regroup at camp and thaw out my feet. Upon arriving there, I brewed coffee. Then John walked up with two shiny rainbows in hand. Dinner was coming, but it was not going to come easily. We snacked for lunch. John had scouted some potential fishing holes and let me in on his findings, rekindling my excitement. Together we ambled upstream in the warm sunshine, spending the balance of the afternoon fishing above the campsite. I pulled a handsome rainbow out of a slow pool flowing past a tall rock ledge below some rapids. The sun left the valley, hastening our return to Lower Ekaneetlee.

We set about our camp chores as suppertime drew near. But our frying pan needed more fish. With determination I grabbed my pole and decided to try a flat riffle in front of the camp. I crawled through a rhododendron thicket between camp and the creek. I caught three trout in succession. What luck! You would have thought that the water near a camp would be hard fished. As I see it, trout rank second only to women as the world's most enigmatic creatures.

Now we were cooking. I immediately cleaned the day's catch with my handy Swiss Army knife. A backpacking cliché, the knife comes in very handy. I prefer the less gadgety models—they are less bulky in your pocket and can fulfill most camp demands, such as cutting rope, opening cans, and cleaning fish. But on expeditions purely to fish, I bring a filet knife also. Lose a knife on the trail, and you will learn how invaluable it is.

I shook the cleaned fish around in a cornmeal-filled freezer bag, then placed them in an oiled frying pan over the camp stove. Soon John and I were eating hot breaded trout on folded newspaper "plates." Fresh trout! The greasy newspapers illuminated our campsite as we threw them in the fire. We sat before the dancing flames in the lee of the Smokies, convincing ourselves that we deserved our own fishing show on TV. John pulled some marshmallows from his pack, and we roasted them. I like mine a melty light brown. He is a marshmallow burner, blowing them out and then eating the blackened sugar goo. Above, the clear, starry sky let the cold in, and by ten o'clock the temperature was in the upper thirties. We fell asleep soon thereafter.

Hours later, I poked my head out of the bag. It was the first day of April. Clear. Cold. Brrr. But the prospect of more trout fishing got me jumping, despite the nippy thirty-degree air. Immediately I was boiling water. After drinking a hot mixture of coffee and hot chocolate, I started up Ekaneetlee Creek on an unmaintained footpath, clad in wet tennis shoes, long socks, shorts, three layers on my upper body, and a wool cap on my head.

FRYING TROUT AT EKANEETLEE CAMPSITE. I shook the fish in a cornmeal-filled freezer bag, then placed them in an oiled frying pan over the camp stove.

They say that the best trout fishing is at dawn. I say that the coldest trout fishing is at dawn. After thirty chilly, luckless minutes of fumbling fingers, snags, and hideous laurel thickets, I returned to camp, having decided to enjoy a warm fire and a hot breakfast. When sleepyhead John noticed that I had revived the fire, he got out of his bag. That is why I call him "Baghdad." The spring sun was working its way down the valley. We ate the rest of the bacon and eggs, with jalapeño corn cakes to absorb the calorie-laden grease.

John packed up his stuff. He was going back to Fontana Dam, an undulating seven-mile hike along a portion of the Lakeshore Trail, then on to Knoxville, a winding sixty-mile drive along Highway 129. After his departure, I cleaned up the campsite and covered my pack with a tarp. I sat in an ever-shifting sunny spot, reading and patiently waiting for the air to warm up.

About 10:30, I again set out up Ekaneetlee Creek. The creek is about one-third the size of Eagle, and its spare banks are profusely overgrown with mountain laurel and rhododendron, beneath a canopy of trees. It is tough to fish that body of water. Precise casting is necessary, and even then an angler should expect to get hung often. That is what happened, of course. But my persistence paid off, as I quickly netted two fat rainbows. I don't use a net, and, when I have little room, I must plan before I cast where I will land the fish once it is hooked. After sloshing my way around a sharp bend, I followed the creek to a place where the valley widened. I cast aside the rod and explored the open area, which was peppered with young trees. Several homesites were in evidence, with rusted wash tubs, mason jars, and squared-off flat spots on the ground.

But man's history along the Ekaneetlee Creek predates the white settlers. Through this valley an ancient Cherokee Indian Trail climbed to the crest of the Smokies at Ekaneetlee Gap, one of the lowest places on the stateline crest, and down along Ekaneetlee Branch into Tennessee. It is awe-inspiring to follow a footpath that is untold years old and has not been obliterated by civilization.

I retrieved my pole and returned to the campsite, recovering my fish along the way. I happily took off my dripping shoes and socks and dried my feet in the nearly seventy-degree air. After a snack, I tied a white Roostertail on my line and ventured up Eagle for more fishing. There is nothing like a spring day that dawns cool and sunny and that you know is going to culminate in a clear, warm bath of sunshine.

I landed a few more fighting trout, returning the smaller ones. The refreshing spring smell in the air was as enjoyable as catching the rainbows, but around four o'clock I called it quits for the day. I cleaned my catch and consigned the guts to Ekaneetlee Creek. It is surprising how rapidly crawfish will devour trout innards. On more than one occasion, I have had crawfish try to steal fish I had cleaned and temporarily stored in a creek.

Another round of fresh fried trout, this time unbreaded, complemented by jalapeño corn cakes, was the evening fare. Alone I read by the fire but lasted little more than an hour before my lids drooped. The night, at forty-eight degrees, was less chilly than the previous one. I shut my eyes, snug in my sleeping bag, and was lulled to sleep by Ekaneetlee and Eagle creeks.

Morning again. I had slept as hard as the rock under my sleeping pad. I buried my head in the bag, shutting out the dawn's early light. Later, when I woke again, it was time to get moving. After reviving the fire, I bolted down a pancake breakfast. The sun was out; its filtered rays dotted the pine-needle campsite floor as I scanned the campsite for overlooked gear. I put on my pack and hustled up the Eagle Creek Trail. A climb of one and four-tenths miles and more fords led me to the Eagle Creek Island campsite (elevation 2,400 feet). Once a logging camp, the site is not a natural island. Early twentieth-century loggers dug a sluice around the location, although it looks completely natural now.

The sun was high above the mountain valley. I loafed around the camp barefoot and shirtless. In the Smokies the first warm days of the year are a real treat for both humans and beasts. The cold grip of winter was loosening. As it had for eons, life in the mountains would begin a new cycle, triggered by the lengthening hours of daylight. After such musings, I got a hankering to fish this stretch of Eagle, which was new to me. The creek, smaller at this elevation, also yielded smaller fish, all of which I released. I was heady with the Smoky Mountain strain of spring fever. As I fished upstream, I came to a deep, circular pool thirty feet in diameter. At its head stood two cabin-sized gray boulders. Between them was a ten-foot fall, over which rushed the waters of the creek. A wary old trout certainly lurked in this pool. I cast repeatedly, to no avail.

I climbed up on one of the boulders to enjoy the scenery at least. In my determination to catch the elusive lunker, I had failed to notice that the sky rapidly was clouding over. Now I heard the pitter-patter of rain in the distance. Deep rumblings emanated from all sides of the valley. A thunderstorm was brewing. I sought refuge under a creekside rhododendron thicket, being a mile or more from the campsite. I had erected no shelter there, anyway. All my gear was lying about exposed. It had been sunny when I left, and in my haste to fish, I had assured myself that no storms would come. Once again, in the outdoors, rain is often one's worst enemy.

The deluge came. Thunder pounded. Lightning flashed. I

sat still in the dusky dark of the coppice, listening to the rain drip all around and onto me. Within half an hour, the sky was clear again. I meandered back to camp, enjoying the bracing air. Surprisingly, the campsite looked as if it had not been hit at all; the leafy floor was dry. The storm had been very restricted in locale.

I discovered that I was virtually out of gas for my stove—poor planning. So I made a small fire of twigs, trying to build up heat quickly, to boil water. It sounds rustic and self-sufficient to use the old campfire for all cooking and heating, and I often grill meat and bake vegetables over the fire. But for other purposes, a stove is much more efficient and easily regulated. The fire cook has to contend with a fire that can be too hot or not hot enough, insuring uneven heat that results in smoke in the eyes, blackened pots, burned fingers, and an angry chef. So there I sat, watching the burning twigs heat the water. An hour after I first gathered sticks, I had boiling water for coffee.

After the java break, I explored the area, finding a patch of tiny purple wildflowers that had sprung up through the fallen leaves. Wildflowers develop particular characteristics to attract insects for pollination, insuring perpetuation of their kind. These flowers were hepatica, which bloom in late March or April at elevations up to three thousand feet. Evidently spring really was on its way.

In the gathering darkness, I again labored over the hot coals, frying more jalapeño corn cakes for supper. The spicy margarine-doused bread sated my hunger. The night was starry and still; the forest stood mute. The bubbling creek and crackling fire were the only sounds that night. It was a moment made for introspection. Seeing the evidence of spring's onset that day had reminded me of my own rebirth in the mountains. Just as spring gave life to the Smokies, the Smokies had given life to me. In my directionless early twenties, I had come to the mountains through a friendship that came about by accident. Now the outdoors in general, and the Smokies in particular, formed the main focus of my life. I felt grateful for all the friendships and the rewarding moments I had found along the way.

By the light of the campfire, I readied myself to sleep in the fifty-degree air. Later I awoke in blackness, chilled from head to toe. A cold front had arrived. My bag had been unzipped when I dozed off, and now I was freezing. Really, it was just above freezing. I zipped up and went back to sleep.

A foggy day dawned on Eagle Creek. I rekindled the fire, warming myself and heating water for hot beverages. After dousing the fire and loading my pack, I set out to cover my final miles on Eagle Creek Trail. Fording a creek in thirty-degree weather is a task to be dreaded. I dreaded it but had to undertake it nonetheless—repeatedly. I would take my boots and socks off, cross, and then put my boots and socks back on. Each time my feet were chilled, then they burned with a strange sensation. During the final phase of this fordathon, I passed a backcountry campsite, Big Walnut.

The last of approximately eighteen fords of Eagle Creek was completed under a cloudy morning sky. The arduous trail now compensated for a lack of fords by becoming ever steeper. Hoarfrost coated the mountainside trees growing above four thousand feet. I crossed a small, rocky streamlet by the name of Spence Cabin Branch, then turned to climb very steeply, arriving at the Spence Field shelter on the Smokies' crest five and a half miles from Eagle Creek Island.

The shelter was cold and dark, the temperature inside twenty-five degrees. The day before, the thermometer had registered seventy degrees. I quickly crossed the windy, frosty field, stopping to take in the view. I stood on mountains that overlooked all of Tennessee. Beneath the cloud cover, flowing curves and peaks stretched off toward the east. Westward, the valley of the Tennessee River lay expansive to the distant Cumberland Mountains, whose ridges went on and on until the skyline melted into the sky itself.

The wind abated on the Bote Mountain Trail, as I descended the mile and a half of Jeep road to the Anthony Creek Trail. The frozen, rocky path pounded my feet during the next three and a half miles to Cades Cove. At the ranger station, I met my prearranged ride home. Though the trip had ended on a chilly note, the season of rebirth had arrived in the valley of the ford.

Bibliographical Essay

One hundred years ago, the Great Smoky Mountains were virtually unknown to the world beyond the range of their now-famous views. In 1904, they were, as Horace Kephart put it, *terra incognita*. In the span of a century, however, unforeseen changes have taken place. For better or for worse, residents of what is now the Great Smoky Mountains National Park were "brought into the twentieth century." After an immense struggle, the logging companies and the settlers were bought out. The national park was established.

Since that time, word of the Smokies' splendor has spread. This park is now the most heavily visited national park in the nation. Such beauty and popularity attracted, and still attract, writers who wax eloquent about everything from bears and salamanders to trails and history. While writing this book, I pored over the plethora of material about the Smokies contained in the library at the University of Tennessee and in books lying about my home. Several sources stood out; others that obviously didn't fit my needs I nonetheless found captivating.

By virtue of being what it is—a book recounting my adventures—*Trial by Trail* should not draw much on other people's writings. In fact, however, in my hiking tales, I have incorporated facts about the mountains' geology, flora, fish, and other features. These facts were gleaned from just such sources.

The human history of the park often remains obscure to the average park visitor. This story—from Indians to settlers to loggers to the fight to establish the park—is what sets the Smokies apart from other beautiful natural areas. The human imprint on

the mountains is as worthy of contemplation as old-growth forest or a crashing hillside cascade. Luckily for us, this living history has been preserved in print. Recorded from the mouths of
those who carved out a living in the hollows beneath Stateline
Ridge, which divides North Carolina and Tennessee, the stories of the mountain folk I read served as a backdrop for my
book. Like the physical presence that the Smokies offer the
visitor, these voices deepen and enrich the experience of all who
come after them in this particular place.

Other aspects of my book, such as the fishing and backpacking tips that can be applied anywhere you can camp and
fish, were distilled from my own experience. Reading books on
"how to backpack" helped to inspire this book. I wanted to share
the tips that I felt were most useful to the average backpacker.
And certain books stimulated my thinking, helping me to see
which ideas best suited my particular style of backpacking. But
the necessity of solving problems in the field remained my most
important teacher.

As a young hellion and later as a park volunteer, I benefited
from the generosity of Park Service employees. They gave me
insight into how the park operates and the reasoning behind
official park policies. The Park Service is a bureaucracy, but it
is made up of individuals, and each one has her or his own ideas.
As a result, along the way I have encountered many different
visions of and for the park.

Here are the books that helped me write *Trial by Trail.*

For up-to-date hard facts about the Smokies, Rose Hook's
Great Smoky Mountains (New York: Houghton Mifflin, 1993),
a natural history guide, was indispensable. It is also very readable. Hook turns a scientific book into a story of the elements
that make up the mountains. The color photographs alone make
the book worth purchasing.

Trees of the Smokies (Gatlinburg, Tenn.: Great Smoky Mountains Natural History Association, 1993) was a handy packet of
information on the true stars of the park. I used it as a refer-
ence to make sure that my discussion of trees was accurate.

Written in 1937 by Laura Thornborough, *The Great Smoky*

Mountains (Knoxville: University of Tennessee Press, 1979) showed me a vision of what the park meant to the generation that fought to create it. This book seems so innocent and optimistic compared to today's writings on the Smokies, which are forced to chronicle so many negative aspects, such as environmental deterioration.

I have used Don Kirk's *Smoky Mountains Trout Fishing Guide* (Birmingham, Ala.: Menasha Ridge Press, 1993) in planning many adventures. His information about Fontana Lake and post-logging trout management provides insight into why certain kinds of fish are where they are.

Colin Fletcher's *The Complete Walker* (New York: Knopf, 1968), though technically outdated, is the best "how to" backpacking book I have encountered. He combines tips with hiking philosophy in a manner that makes you want to get out on the trail.

If you read any fair amount of Smokies literature, you will encounter Horace Kephart. This chronicler of the "back of beyond" ironically wound up being part of Smokies history himself. His book *Our Southern Highlanders* (Knoxville: University of Tennessee Press, 1984) is *the* preeminent volume on mountain people of the Smokies before the park's establishment. This timeless book convinced me to emphasize the park's historical uniqueness. Another book by Kephart, *Camping and Woodcraft* (Knoxville: University of Tennessee Press, 1988) actually was written by candlelight in a cabin in the Smokies, when the author first arrived there at the turn of the century. Using examples from his Smokies experiences, Kephart offers advice for the outdoors adventurers of his era and for me as well.

Strangers in High Places, by Michael Frome (Knoxville: University of Tennessee Press, 1994), narrates the history of these Southern Highlands. Another highly readable, fact-filled book, it details the evolution of the Smokies from the land of the Cherokee to the national park it is today.

The current authority on the Smokies, Carson Brewer, has written many books on the Smokies, but my favorite is *A Wonderment of Mountains: The Great Smokies* (Knoxville, Tenn.:

Tenpenny Publishing, 1981). The mountain lore and other observations on the Smokies helped me select what I thought would be most interesting to the readers of *Trial by Trail*.

Each of these books contributed to my book in its own special way. No matter what you read about the Smokies, you come away with the feeling that the Smokies are not just a collection of mountains. Rather they constitute a unique canvas upon which has been painted a picture of people interacting with their environment in good, bad, and indifferent ways.